ARISTOCRATS AND ARCHAEOLOGISTS

ARISTOCRATS AND ARCHAEOLOGISTS

An Edwardian Journey on the Nile

TOBY WILKINSON
JULIAN PLATT

The American University in Cairo Press
Cairo New York

Exclusive distribution outside Egypt and North America by I.B.Tauris & Co Ltd., 6 Salem Road, London, W2 4BU

Dar el Kutub No. 26188/16
ISBN 978 977 416 845 1

Dar el Kutub Cataloging-in-Publication Data

Wilkinson, Toby
    Aristocrats and Archaeologists: An Edwardian Journey on the Nile / Toby Wilkinson and Julian Platt.—Cairo: The American University in Cairo Press, 2017.
        p.   cm.
        ISBN: 978 977 416 845 1
        1. Egypt—Description and travel
        2. Archaeologists—Biography
        I.   Platt, Julian (jt. auth.)
        916.2

1 2 3 4 5   21 20 19 18 17

Designed by Sally Boylan
Printed in the United States of America

For

Amanda
a good friend to Violet

Claudie and Damian
Ferdy's great-great-niece and -nephew

Daisy, Alfred, and Constance
Ferdy's great-great-great-nieces and -nephew

and for
Michael Bailey

Contents

Map of the Journey

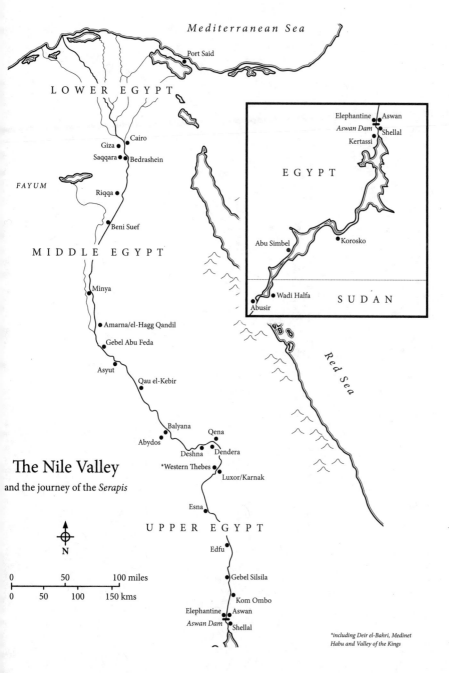

Mediterranean Sea

LOWER EGYPT

Port Said

Cairo
Giza
Saqqara ● ● Bedrashein

FAYUM

Riqqa

Beni Suef

MIDDLE EGYPT

Minya

Amarna/el-Hagg Qandil

Gebel Abu Feda

Asyut

Qau el-Kebir

Balyana
Qena
Abydos
Deshna Dendera
*Western Thebes
Luxor/Karnak

Esna

UPPER EGYPT

Edfu

Gebel Silsila

Kom Ombo
Elephantine ● ● Aswan
Aswan Dam ● Shellal

The Nile Valley
and the journey of the *Serapis*

0   50   100 miles
0   50   100   150 kms

N

Red Sea

Elephantine ● ● Aswan
Aswan Dam ● Shellal
Kertassi

E G Y P T

Abu Simbel ● ● Korosko

Wadi Halfa
Abusir

S U D A N

*including Deir el-Bahri, Medinet
Habu and Valley of the Kings*

The Itinerary

The voyage upstream

Date	Remarks, visits, meetings	Overnight mooring
Thursday, November 7, 1907	Departed Cairo	Bedrashein
Friday, November 8	Saqqara, Quibell	Bedrashein
Saturday, November 9		Riqqa
Sunday, November 10–		
Monday, November 11		Beni Suef
Tuesday, November 12		Off Sharua, north of Minya
Wednesday, November 13		el-Hagg Qandil
Thursday, November 14	Amarna	Gebel Abu Feda
Friday, November 15	Asyut	Asyut
Saturday, November 16		Qau el-Kebir
Sunday, November 17–		
Monday, November 18		Between Qau and Balyana
Tuesday, November 19	Abydos	Between Qau and Balyana
Wednesday, November 20		5 miles from Balyana
Thursday, November 21	Dendera	Between Qena and Luxor
Friday, November 22	Arrived in Luxor;	
	Karnak by moonlight	Luxor

Date	Remarks, visits, meetings	Overnight mooring
Saturday, November 23	Karnak, Legrain	Luxor
Sunday, November 24	Deir el-Bahri, Weigall	Luxor
Monday, November 25	Medinet Habu	Luxor
Tuesday, November 26		Luxor
Wednesday, November 27	Valley of the Kings, Ayrton	Luxor
Thursday, November 28–		
Sunday, December 1		Luxor
Monday, December 2	Departed Luxor	Esna
Tuesday, December 3	Esna barrage, Mr. Lloyd	Esna
Wednesday, December 4	Edfu pylon	Edfu
Thursday, December 5	Gebel al-Silsila quarries	Gebel al-Silsila
Friday, December 6	Irrigation works,	
	Birch, Willcocks	Kom Ombo
Saturday, December 7		Kom Ombo
Sunday, December 8	Arrived in Aswan	Aswan
Monday, December 9		Aswan
Tuesday, December 10	Elephantine, Gardiner	Aswan
Wednesday, December 11–		
Thursday, December 12		Aswan
Friday, December 13	Hesseh, Reisner,	
	and Elliot Smith	Aswan
Saturday, December 14–		
Saturday, December 28		Aswan
Sunday, December 29	Churchill, departed Aswan	Kertassi
Monday, December 30		Shellal
Tuesday, December 31		Korosko
Wednesday, January 1, 1908	Abu Simbel	Between Abu Simbel and
		Wadi Halfa
Thursday, January 2	Arrived in Wadi Halfa	Wadi Halfa
Friday, January 3	Donkey ride	Wadi Halfa
Saturday, January 4	Rock of Abusir	Wadi Halfa

The voyage downstream

Date	Remarks, visits, meetings	Overnight mooring
Sunday, January 5, 1908	Departed Wadi Halfa	Between Wadi Halfa and Abu Simbel
Monday, January 6		Korosko
Tuesday, January 7		Shellal
Wednesday, January 8	Arrived in Aswan	Aswan
Thursday, January 9		Aswan
Friday, January 10	Tea at Savoy, Sir S. MacKenzie	Aswan
Saturday, January 11– Sunday, January 12		Aswan
Monday, January 13	Sayce	Aswan
Tuesday, January 14	Departed Aswan	Kom Ombo
Wednesday, January 15	Arrived in Luxor	Luxor
Thursday, January 16– Saturday, January 18		Luxor
Sunday, January 19	Thebes, Carter	Luxor
Monday, January 20	Cliffs behind Deir el-Bahri, lunch with Carter, tomb of Nefertari	Luxor
Tuesday, January 21– Saturday, January 25		Luxor
Sunday, January 26	Departed Luxor	Deshna
Monday, January 27	Abydos	Balyana
Tuesday, January 28– Thursday, January 30		Between Balyana and Riqqa
Friday, January 31		Riqqa
Saturday, February 1	Arrived in Cairo, tea at Shepheard's	Cairo
Sunday, February 2	Egyptian Museum	Cairo
Monday, February 3	Departed Cairo	Port Said
Tuesday, February 4	Embarked SS *Mongolia*	At sea
Saturday, February 15	Disembarked SS *Mongolia*	Home

Family Trees

(not comprehensive, and listing only those relevant to this story)

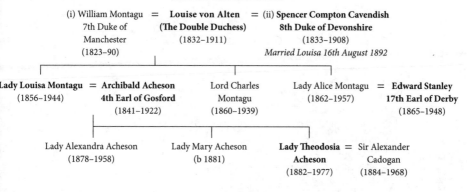

THE DEVONSHIRE PARTY

(i) William Montagu = **Louise von Alten** = (ii) **Spencer Compton Cavendish**
7th Duke of **(The Double Duchess)** **8th Duke of Devonshire**
Manchester (1832–1911) (1833–1908)
(1823–90) *Married Louisa 16th August 1892*

Lady Louisa Montagu = **Archibald Acheson**   Lord Charles   Lady Alice Montagu = **Edward Stanley**
(1856–1944) **4th Earl of Gosford** Montagu (1862–1957) **17th Earl of Derby**
(1841–1922) (1860–1939) (1865–1948)

Lady Alexandra Acheson   Lady Mary Acheson   **Lady Theodosia** = Sir Alexander
(1878–1958) (b 1881) **Acheson** Cadogan
(1882–1977) (1884–1968)

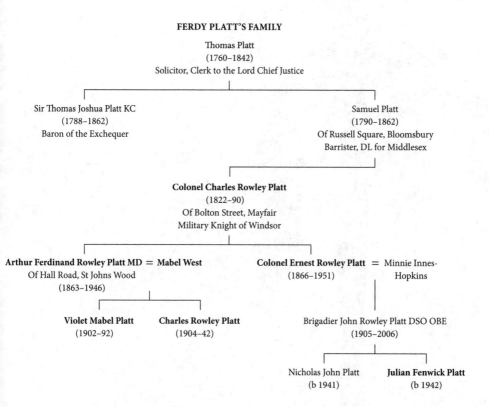

FERDY PLATT'S FAMILY

Thomas Platt
(1760–1842)
Solicitor, Clerk to the Lord Chief Justice

Sir Thomas Joshua Platt KC   Samuel Platt
(1788–1862) (1790–1862)
Baron of the Exchequer Of Russell Square, Bloomsbury
Barrister, DL for Middlesex

Colonel Charles Rowley Platt
(1822–90)
Of Bolton Street, Mayfair
Military Knight of Windsor

Arthur Ferdinand Rowley Platt MD = Mabel West   **Colonel Ernest Rowley Platt** = Minnie Innes-
Of Hall Road, St Johns Wood (1866–1951) Hopkins
(1863–1946)

Violet Mabel Platt   **Charles Rowley Platt**   Brigadier John Rowley Platt DSO OBE
(1902–92) (1904–42) (1905–2006)

Nicholas John Platt   **Julian Fenwick Platt**
(b 1941) (b 1942)

I

An Introduction to Ferdy's Tale

by Toby Wilkinson

T his book tells the story of an Edwardian journey on the Nile in the winter of 1907–1908. At its core is a remarkable series of letters which provide a first-hand account of the three-month trip—the sites visited, the passengers aboard and the people encountered ashore, the clashes of culture and of class. More than a mere travelogue, this correspondence from over a century ago opens a window on the rarefied worlds of aristocracy and archaeology during their golden age. What emerges is a vivid picture of privilege and adventure that continues to enthrall.

Ferdy's letters

In 2006, I met Julian Platt at a college reunion. On learning that I was an Egyptologist, Julian mentioned a collection of letters he had inherited from his cousin and godmother Violet. They had been written by Violet's father, Ferdy, during a trip up the Nile in the early twentieth century. Would I be interested in reading them? They sounded intriguing. Yes, I replied.

The loose bundle of letters arrived in a padded envelope, together with photographs of the small, painted box in which they had been stored for decades. There was no doubt that the maker of the box had been an accomplished artist:

the scenes on the long sides were faithful reproductions of ancient Egyptian tomb paintings. But what really caught my eye were the hieroglyphic inscriptions painted on the two short sides of the box: no mere jumble of random signs, they looked like well-crafted sentences. Indeed, one inscription read,

> Year 13 month 8 day 30 under the Majesty of George, fifth of that name. Says the physician Ferdinand, "Behold, I have painted this box with my own hand for my daughter whom I love, Violet. I did this in order that my memory may remain firm in the heart of my daughter and that my name may be in her mouth."

while the second inscription stated,

> Behold, this box belongs to the maiden Violet. Her mother was the mistress of the house Mabel; her father the physician Ferdinand. He says, "I have spoken with words of magical power over this box. If anyone injures it or damages the writing upon it, my curse shall reach them wherever they may be."

This was my first introduction to A.F.R. Platt, the writer of the letters that had been kept, forgotten and unread, in his hand-made box for so long. All I knew, from Julian, was that "great uncle Ferdy" had made the box for his daughter as a memento on his return from Egypt. His account of the trip, undertaken as private physician to the Duke of Devonshire, was contained in the letters he had written home to his wife Mabel (May) every few days, during his long sojourn in the Nile Valley.

It was immediately clear that Egypt must have made more than a passing impression on Ferdy: the painted box showed a keen appreciation of ancient Egyptian art, while the inscriptions, accurately rendered in grammatically correct ancient Egyptian, indicated a near-professional knowledge of hieroglyphic writing. "The physician Ferdinand" had clearly been an amateur Egyptologist of some distinction, but my first reaction was that his letters home would perhaps be unlikely to hold much interest a century later.

Yet, as I opened the bundle of correspondence and started to read, Ferdy's words leapt off the page and began to fire my imagination. His letters—carefully inscribed on sheets from a "Medieval Cream wove bank writing tablet" until it ran out in furthest Nubia—brought vividly to life a lost world: of Edwardian travel, of Egypt on the brink of the modern age, of the great figures of Egyptology, of aristocrats and archaeologists. Ferdy's letters were nothing less than a time capsule, a rich evocation of a vanished era, a first-hand account of the Edwardians' encounter with Egypt. As I read on, it was clear that Ferdy's letters also revealed his private thoughts, the intimate feelings of the man behind the professional exterior. Here, in short, was a correspondence of rare scope and richness. It clearly deserved a wider readership.

A golden age of travel

Ferdy's trip up the Nile took place in the winter of 1907–1908, during the golden age of travel to Egypt. Edwardian England was still a country where tuberculosis and other respiratory diseases, exacerbated by the smogs and the cold, dank winter weather, claimed innumerable lives. To escape such threats to their health, the leisured aristocratic class had, for a long time, taken to spending the winter months in warmer, sunnier climes. Britain's colonial possessions of India and South Africa were natural destinations, until the opening up of Egypt to Western visitors in the mid-nineteenth century provided an equally attractive winter destination, much closer to home.

The Victorian popular novelist Amelia Edwards's 1870s best seller, *A Thousand Miles Up the Nile*, brought the wonders of ancient Egypt to a mass readership, initiating a love of Nile cruising that has never abated. While Thomas Cook brought trips up the Nile within reach of the middle classes, for the wealthy the preferred means of conveyance remained the privately hired houseboat (*dahabiya*) or, from the 1890s, the faster steamship. Rented from the port of Cairo, complete with crew and servants, a private *dahabiya* or steamer provided a comfortable home-away-from-home on which aristocratic travelers could relax and entertain on their journey up the Nile.

Even with such luxurious surroundings, however, there was no escaping the trials and tribulations faced by all travelers to Egypt, then and now. Ferdy's letters talk of dust storms and diarrhea, of wild fluctuations in temperature (boiling hot one day, freezing cold the next), and of the persistent menace of mosquitoes and midges: "We have been horribly bitten and the irritation is disagreeable." Moreover, the steamer, although much faster than a sailing boat, was noisy and dirty: "The shaking of the ship by day and the dynamo which works the electric light is rather trying."

On a Cook's tour, a visitor could see all the main sights of Egypt on a two- or three-week return trip from London. But for the well-heeled tourist with a private income and no need to hurry back, the done thing was to spend the whole of the winter in Egypt, sailing from Cairo to Wadi Halfa and back again, a trip of some three months. Add to that the journey from London to Cairo (by boat or train to Brindisi, by steamer to Port Said, and thence by train to Cairo) and the return leg, and a traveler could expect to be away from England from the beginning of November to the middle of February, thus avoiding virtually the whole of the cold and unhealthy European winter.

Such was the journey undertaken by the Duke and Duchess of Devonshire; their relations Lord and Lady Gosford; one of the Gosfords' daughters, Lady Theo; the duke's friend Sir Charles Cradock-Hartopp; and the duke's private physician A.F.R. Platt in the winter of 1907–1908. They left England in late October and arrived at the port of Cairo in the first week of November, where their boat, the steamer SS *Serapis*, was being made ready. Once all the formalities had been accomplished, the party embarked on Thursday, November 7, and set sail southward, against the current, but conveyed gently along by the prevailing northerly wind. The journey from Cairo to Luxor took two full weeks, with overnight stops at major points of interest along the way, including Bedrashein for the pyramids of Saqqara, Minya for the tombs of Beni Hasan, el-Hagg Qandil for the ruined city of Amarna, and Balyana for the temples of Abydos. On arrival at Luxor, Ferdy and his companions stayed for ten days, exploring the monuments of ancient Thebes, before continuing their journey south, via Esna, Edfu, and Kom Ombo (still the highlights of a modern Nile cruise) to the southern city of Aswan. There they stayed three weeks over the Christmas period, enjoying the dry, sunny climate and exploring the marvels, ancient and modern, of the Cataract region. From Aswan, the journey into Nubia took just four days, including New Year's Day 1908 close to the great riverside temples of Abu Simbel. After a brief, three-day stop at Wadi Halfa in Anglo-Egyptian Sudan, they turned around and headed back north, this time buoyed along by the Nile's current.

Three days later they were back in Aswan, for a shorter five-day sojourn before retracing their steps to Luxor for a further ten-day stay. Finally, on Sunday, January 26, they slipped their moorings and started the final leg northward, arriving in Cairo the following weekend. A couple of days later found Ferdy in Port Said, embarking the SS *Mongolia* for the ten-day voyage back to England, via Marseilles and the Straits of Gibraltar. When he walked through his front door in London, Ferdy had been away from home—away from his wife and children—for the best part of four months.

The class divide

Attending to aloof aristocrats was a necessary part of the job of a personal physician, but spending a quarter of a year cooped up with the Devonshires and their blue-blooded friends on a boat on the Nile proved a trying experience. Ferdy's was a world of maids and middle-class comfort, enlivened by a love of learning and literature (during his trip up the Nile, he is reading *Kipps* by H.G. Wells while, back home in London, his wife is reading *Tristram Shandy*). It was a world away from his patron's life at Chatsworth or Devonshire House. One of the most fascinating aspects of Ferdy's letters home to his wife May is his acute observation of his aristocratic traveling companions and the mores of the time—a rarefied world of privilege, protocol, and "pudding à la royale," as depicted in the television series *Downton Abbey*.

The duke was an invalid, and had gone to Egypt for his health. Although he had a natural distrust for doctors, he evidently had confidence in Ferdy, and also liked to quiz his well-read physician about Egyptology and astronomy. However, a mild aristocratic interest in the civilization of the pharaohs did not extend to sensitivity toward modern Egypt's or its customs. The Devonshires and their party kept up the lifestyle of an English country house—shooting game, dressing for dinner, drinking champagne, and playing bridge—seemingly oblivious to their Nilotic surroundings. Even Ferdy found it somewhat incongruous to see the duchess walking through the streets of Minya "dressed in white flannel with a big bunch of artificial violets . . . and a white flat hat." The duke was unable to walk, due to his infirmity, so was accustomed to being carried in a palanquin, like an oriental potentate.

By comparison with the exotic sights and sounds on shore, Ferdy found life on board the *Serapis* rather boring. The duchess spoke only "sparingly," and Lady Theo was "supercilious and chilling," while Lord Gosford and Sir Charles were bossy and condescending. The duke, too, was a man of few words. Breeding and learning were two very different things, and, as time went by, Ferdy found his companions' limited conversation—their "well-bred indifference"—increasingly enervating. Whenever he could, he escaped the claustrophobic confines of the boat and went for long walks in the desert, finding solace in his own company. Just two weeks into the trip, Ferdy wrote rather wistfully, "I am looking forward to Luxor where we shall probably stay some days, as I shall be able to see more."

This homesickness, somewhat unexpected in a professional London physician, is a notable feature of Ferdy's letters. As he headed further and further upstream, away from London and into the heart of Africa, his thoughts turned increasingly to home. On first going aboard the *Serapis*, Ferdy was full of excitement at being back in Egypt, a country he had first visited as a young man in 1896, before his marriage, and which had evidently kindled a lifelong fascination. But as the days went by, he started to miss his wife and children. After only ten days afloat, Ferdy wrote, "It seems months since I left home and I begin to wish myself back again. I should like to pop in suddenly and see what you and the chicks are doing." While Ferdy had ample opportunity to write, and dispatched a letter back to London every few days, May was no doubt busy with the household and children, and had less time for correspondence. Deliveries of mail to Egypt were altogether less reliable than the outbound service, and the paucity of letters from home only exacerbated Ferdy's feelings of loneliness and separation.

Another effect of distance was the stripping away of Ferdy's usual Edwardian reserve. In the letters written at the beginning of his journey, Ferdy signs himself "A.F.R. Platt" with all the formality of a respectable London physician. A week in, he feels liberated enough to add ten kisses after his name. Five days later, on reaching Upper Egypt, the formal "A.F.R. Platt" has become "Ferdy (A.F.R. Platt)" with ten kisses for each of his children. By January 11, over a month into the trip, the formal style disappears entirely, and he is simply "Your ever loving husband Ferdy." Then, as the journey home begins, the formality starts to return. Back in Luxor, at the end of January, he is "A.F.R. Platt (Ferdy)" again, and, on disembarking in Cairo, plain "A.F.R. Platt." Far from home, Ferdy felt able to escape the conventions of Edwardian society and give voice to his human emotions. This is one of the most compelling aspects of his letters.

Aristocrats and archaeologists

The first decade of the twentieth century was a golden age of Egyptology, when wealthy patrons and Western museums were competing with each other to sponsor excavations the length and breadth of the Nile Valley, leading to a transformation in the understanding of ancient Egyptian civilization. The very month that the Duke of Devonshire's party arrived in Egypt, another English aristocrat, the Earl of Carnarvon, was beginning his excavations in western Thebes—the start of a campaign that would result, fifteen years later, in the discovery of the tomb of Tutankhamun. Had the duke been more interested in antiquities, he and Ferdy might easily have met Carnarvon in Luxor.

Although the Duke of Devonshire had only a passing interest in antiquities, and some of his party were altogether indifferent to Egypt's ancient culture, Ferdy was fascinated by Egyptology—a legacy of his 1896 visit—and took a keen interest in the monuments and the ongoing archaeological work. As well as visiting the major sites, he sought out archaeologists to learn about the latest discoveries, and in doing so met many of the greatest figures in the history of Egyptology. His letters provide a fascinating snapshot of Egyptian archaeology at its zenith.

At Saqqara, Ferdy met the English archaeologist James Quibell, who was working on a Coptic monastery as well as at the Step Pyramid and in the surrounding cemetery. The Devonshire party visited a newly discovered tomb where some human remains had been found; Lady Gosford "took away a piece of a lower jaw with 3 teeth for the Duchess." On the way south to Luxor, they visited the ruined city of the heretic pharaoh Akhenaten at Amarna, which had only recently been revealed through the excavations of Flinders Petrie. One of its great attractions, a painted pavement in the royal palace, was the highlight of the visit.

On more than one occasion, Ferdy was struck by the pace of excavation since his first visit to Egypt a decade earlier. The temple of Dendera had been cleared from the sand of centuries, while the ancient monuments of Thebes were a hive of archaeological activity. Medinet Habu and Karnak had been largely cleared, too, and artists were hard at work recording the reliefs and sculptures at the temple of Hatshepsut at Deir el-Bahri. Here, Ferdy was shown around by Arthur Weigall, inspector of antiquities for Upper Egypt. In the Valley of the Kings, Ferdy's guide was Edward Ayrton, an English archaeologist in the employ of the wealthy American patron Theodore M. Davis, who held the concession for the royal necropolis. Ferdy noted drily that "[Ayrton] does all the hard work and Davis gets the credit," before adding, "It was an interesting day for me as so many fresh tombs had been opened since '96 when I was here before." Davis would continue to sponsor excavations in the Valley of the Kings for another seven years before declaring the site "exhausted," thus paving the way for another patron-and-archaeologist pairing, the Earl of Carnarvon and Howard Carter, to make their famous discovery.

Moving on to Aswan, Ferdy met Alan Gardiner—then still a young scholar, but later to become one of the most famous Egyptologists of the twentieth century; the great American archaeologist George Andrew Reisner, whom Ferdy found "rather abrupt and not highly polished"; and the venerable Oxford professor Archibald Sayce, who would soon sell his beloved *dahabiya*, professing Egypt spoiled by modernization. In a further indication of Ferdy's keen interest in ancient Egypt, he showed Sayce an academic paper he had written; Sayce suggested submitting it for publication by the Society of Biblical Archaeology, the preeminent academic body in the field.

When the *Serapis* moored at Luxor for a second time, on the way back to Cairo, Ferdy could not resist visiting the temples of Luxor and Karnak twice each. The highlight of his trip, though, was spending time with Howard Carter, whom Ferdy had met in 1896, and who had since been fired from his job at the Antiquities Service and gone back to painting. Carter took Ferdy to the top of the mountain behind Deir el-Bahri; the two lunched together at Carter's house before visiting the tomb of Queen Nefertari in the Valley of the Queens, which Carter had painted. Ferdy noted Carter's skill as an artist, declaring, "If I had the money spare I would buy this particular picture without a moment's hesitation." At Ferdy's recommendation, the Duke of Devonshire bought two of Carter's paintings the following day, thus helping the impecunious archaeologist to eke out a living until his propitious engagement with Lord Carnarvon later that very year.

During his three months on the Nile, Ferdy thus met many of the giants of Egyptology—some in their prime, others yet to achieve fame. But perhaps the most notable encounter of the whole trip was with a man destined for greatness in another field of endeavour entirely. As the *Serapis* left Aswan for Wadi Halfa on Sunday, December 29, 1907, "Winston Churchill on board a steamer came down the river on his way back from Uganda." Ferdy noted how odd it was that his brother Erny had met Churchill in the Khyber Pass ten years previously, "and now I have met him at the 1st Cataract." Only in Egypt in the first decade of the twentieth century could someone bump into Winston Churchill and Howard Carter within the space of three weeks.

Ferdy's remarkable letters thus combine history, geography, travel, social commentary, and autobiography. They include eloquent descriptions of Egypt's ancient monuments and its modern transformation; acute reflections on the class divide; and amusing pen portraits of famous aristocrats and archaeologists. Forgotten and unread for a century, the correspondence of an unknown London physician unexpectedly brings to life the collision of two remarkable worlds—Edwardian high society (supremely self-assured, yet unknowingly sleepwalking toward extinction) and the Nile Valley, itself poised between its ancient past and an uncertain future. A.F.R. Platt's correspondence from Egypt—like the container in which it languished for so long—is truly a box of delights.

2

The Setting for the Voyage

The Allure and Fashion of Egypt

Thomas Cook and the birth of Egyptian tourism

The first Englishman to travel up the Nile was Richard Pococke, an Anglican clergyman, who visited Egypt in the winter of 1737–38. He hired a *dahabiya* to take him upstream all the way to the First Nile Cataract, thus setting the trend for subsequent generations of tourists. The published account of Pococke's travels, *A Description of the East and Some Other Countries* (1743), contained the first drawings and descriptions of many of Egypt's major monuments, but it was not until the Napoleonic expedition of 1798 that popular interest in pharaonic civilization began in earnest in the Western world.

Nelson's victory over the French at the Battle of the Nile, together with the publication of the monumental *Description de l'Égypte* (1809–1829), and the decipherment of hieroglyphics by Jean-François Champollion in 1822, all fed a growing fascination with the Nile and its ancient civilization. A steady flow of European travelers made their way to Egypt, often as part of a wider tour of the Holy Land. Most tourists, including Florence Nightingale in 1849, chose to hire a *dahabiya* to sail up the Nile, and at the start of the winter season some two or three hundred craft could be found moored up at Bulaq, the main river port of Cairo, awaiting hire.

By the second half of the nineteenth century, Egypt had established itself as a fashionable winter resort for the wealthy. The Prince of Wales (the future King Edward VII) took a trip up the Nile in 1862 and liked it so much that he returned six years later, giving the country a royal seal of approval. The grand opening of the Suez Canal in 1869 enhanced Egypt's international profile and further stimulated demand for Nile travel. And an entrepreneur named Thomas Cook from the English Midlands saw the opportunity to make money from Egyptian tourism, and in so doing changed the face of Nile travel—and of Egypt—forever.

Before 1869, the only means of traveling up the Nile was by privately hired *dahabiya* (an expensive option, reserved for the well-to-do) or by commercial steamer (an erratic and unpredictable service). So that year, Thomas Cook of Leicester chartered two small steamships for the first publically advertised cruise from Cairo to Aswan and back. The following January, his son John Mason Cook hired from the Egyptian government a larger steamer, with beds for forty-four guests, and "personally conducted to the First Cataract and back the largest party of English and American tourists that had to that date ascended the river as one party." The trip was a great success, and by the autumn of 1870, Cook's had been granted the sole agency for a passenger service by Nile steamer.

Prospective tourists were now able to avail themselves of a regular, reliable fortnightly service from Cairo to Wadi Halfa and back, calling at points of interest at fixed dates—and all for a fixed price. What had previously taken two or three months by *dahabiya* could now be accomplished by steamer in three weeks, bringing Nile tourism within reach of the salaried middle classes. That first season of 1870, three hundred American tourists registered at the US Consulate in Cairo before embarking on an Egyptian cruise.

This growing number of visitors stimulated further developments, both inside and outside Egypt. A new steamship service was introduced between Brindisi in southern Italy and Alexandria, cutting the journey time to just three-and-a-half days, while a railway line from Alexandria to Cairo vastly improved internal communications. In 1877, Cook's opened the first hotel in Luxor, and the company had offices in all the principal towns along the Nile Valley, where tourists could send and receive mail and make onward travel arrangements. In Cairo, carriages were laid on for the excursion to the pyramids, and official guides were provided at all the major sites throughout Egypt. Tourism as we know it today had arrived.

Wintering in Egypt

The early European visitors to Egypt in the mid-nineteenth century were struck as much by its benign climate as by its ancient monuments. The enchanting watercolors of Egypt, full of golden hues, painted by David Roberts, and his favorable comparison of the Nile Valley sunsets with the miserable fogs of London, struck a particular chord with the inhabitants of Britain and America—especially those who suffered from tuberculosis or other respiratory conditions. The leisured classes, with time and money to spend, generally emigrated to warmer, foreign climes for the winter months.

Cook's success, and the resulting expansion of Egyptian tourism, tapped into this lucrative market. Luxor, with its ancient monuments, picturesque scenery, and dry climate, was marketed as the quintessential health resort, "the ultimate goal of many who sought to escape the rigours of the Continental and English winters." Lucie Duff Gordon's seven years at Thebes (1862–69), occasioned by her own tuberculosis, and her letters home popularized Upper Egypt as a destination for fellow sufferers. The introduction of a wagon-lit service from Cairo to Luxor made Upper Egypt easily accessible by rail, obviating the need for a lengthy Nile voyage.

From the 1870s to the outbreak of the First World War, every winter from late November to the end of March, consumptive aristocrats and arthritic financiers abandoned their cold, damp, foggy homes in London or New York for the clear blue skies and warm dry air of the Nile Valley. Staying at Luxor in 1881, one Englishman could not quite believe the improvement in his health: "In about a week the sunshine and warm air of Luxor enabled me to sit in the garden, in another week I could mount a donkey, in a month I was able to ride to Karnak. . . . Upon me, at all events, the effect of the climate was little short of miraculous."[1]

Luxor in the winter season began to attract an eclectic, well-heeled clientele, with an emphasis on aristocrats and archaeologists. One of the most prominent figures was the Reverend Archibald Sayce, Professor of Assyriology at the University of Oxford. Of his first visit to Egypt in the early 1880s, he wrote, "Every day was a fresh revelation to me, the cloudless skies and warm air . . . gave me a sensation of life such as I had never felt before, and for the first time since I was born I found it a pleasure to live for the mere sake of living."[2] So taken was he with life on the Nile, that in 1891 he resigned his chair at Oxford and his teaching duties, moved to Egypt, and bought a *dahabiya*. Thereafter, for the next eighteen years, he spent every winter on the

Nile, copying inscriptions, meeting fellow Egyptologists, and entertaining various aristocratic visitors.

For those tourists who hankered after a little more comfort than could be found on a houseboat, the opening of a new grand hotel on the Luxor corniche, the Winter Palace, in 1907 offered a home away from home, "a magnificent hotel fitted with all the luxuries of the age." Its kitchen and bathroom arrangements were singled out for particular praise. One of the hotel's clients that first season was the Earl of Carnarvon, who had taken to wintering in Egypt in 1903 after a motoring accident had left him disabled and prone to bouts of rheumatic pain in his legs. Carnarvon quickly developed an interest in Egypt's ancient past; his meeting, in 1907, with the brilliant but irascible Howard Carter forged a partnership between aristocrat and archaeologist that would result, fifteen years later, in the greatest archaeological discovery of all time.

Also spending time in Egypt that winter of 1907–1908—though on a *dahabiya* rather than at the Winter Palace—was another aristocrat, the Duke of Devonshire, and his personal physician–cum–amateur Egyptologist, Ferdy Platt. The lasting legacy of their trip up the Nile was not a major archaeological discovery, but a treasure trove of correspondence.

The Passengers aboard the *Serapis*

Earlier experiences of Egypt

Neither the Duke of Devonshire nor his personal physician were strangers to the Nile, but in the winter of 1907–1908, it was the duke's declining health and the need for a restorative three-month trip to Egypt that had brought together the two of them and the other passengers of the *dahabiya Serapis*.

There is no record of how Dr. Arthur Ferdinand Rowley Platt of 18 Hall Road London NW8, known to his friends as "Ferdy," came to be appointed to the intimate role of personal physician. However, it would seem likely that the duke's agents would have sought to locate a highly regarded physician with a serious knowledge of Egyptology, who could attend both to the duke's physical ailments and to his intellectual curiosity. This may have been through the personal columns of the *Times* or the membership of the influential Egypt Exploration Fund,[3] whose London exhibitions Ferdy, as he reveals in his letters, frequently attended.

The duke in all likelihood acquired the genuine interest in Egyptology that Ferdy later records during an earlier visit made in 1890, again to recuperate from congestion of the lungs. On that occasion he also traveled the Nile, on the maiden voyage of the *dahabiya Nepthis,* in the company of his later companions, the Earl and Countess of Gosford—close friends who by 1907 would have become his step-daughter and son-in-law. In the archive at Chatsworth, the Derbyshire seat of the Dukes of Devonshire, there is a long letter from the Countess Louisa to her sister recounting her attempts at photographing the expedition's crew, amid the "persecution" of mosquitoes. "Yesterday the crew were given their clothes—white, baggy linen trousers and loose shirts and striped red waistcoats—they got into them on all parts of the deck, one chose a nice secluded spot on the top of the cook's galley—it was very funny to see their look of self-consciousness and pleased vanity, as each one appeared before his friends!"

Both the *Serapis* and the *Nepthis* were luxury *dahabiya*s, fit for grand aristocratic parties. The *Serapis* was a small private steamer with ten cabins for fifteen passengers, two staterooms, a dining salon, and smoking room. By contrast, when Ferdy first voyaged on the Nile in 1896, he did so aboard the *Rameses*, a first-class paddle steamer which was configured to accommodate seventy passengers and was at the time the largest vessel in the Nile fleet of Thomas Cook & Son.

While the aristocratic and leisured classes approached their Egyptian travels for the most part as cultured tourists, following the fashion of their age, there is no doubt that Ferdy pursued his first visit with a passion and intensity of interest that was to last his lifetime. He had set out in 1896, a bachelor of thirty-three and with an apparently wealthy companion he referred to only as "Reiss," on a four-month Mediterranean sojourn to Egypt by way of Paris, Turin, Brindisi, and Alexandria. In his letters to his mother and brother Erny, which were also contained in Violet's box, he had been a keen, and sometimes acerbic, observer of the worlds that passed by him.

Paris had been the gateway to this first Middle Eastern adventure:

> After a four hours journey through very uninteresting country we reached Paris very punctually at seven pm. We had very little trouble at their Custom examination as they did not even look at our luggage, so we drove to the grand Hotel, an impressive building in the Boulevard des Capucines. After a wash and dressing we had an excellent dinner at the restaurant belonging to the Hotel and then all went to a sort of huge music hall, with a variety entertainment which was rather uninteresting but which gave one a good idea of the sort of life Parisians

lead. We were very lucky too in that there was a sort of carnival going on which was amusing to watch. They threw confetti and lay paper ribbons about just as one reads of their doing in Italy at Carnival time, and they had a strange procession headed by a brass band which reminded me of a pantomime – huge vegetables with human faces and most absurd expressions – carrots, turnips, cabbages, cauliflowers, artichokes, aspar- agus etc. etc. I saw them dance the Can-Can for the first time and we left them still at it at 12.45am. I came away with the impression that the French are overgrown children. One thing however I must say, there was no drunkenness and although they were very noisy and lively there were no rows, which would certainly have occurred in England. The French soldier is a poor mess to use a Yorkshire expression. I am pleased with the broad streets and fine boulevards and the Louvre which would give one food for reflection and study for six months at least.

On the journey much letter space was given to the attractions of the food and wine encountered. "They gave us a very good dinner at the hotel at Turin where we stayed for four hours. They gave us thistles stewed in some sauce and they were uncommonly good. As also were some game croquettes. We tried some Italian wine called Barbera which I liked." However, unfortunately, he found "the Italians are a dirty lot and reek of garlic." Compensated by "the famous Bologna sausages," the twenty-seven-hour journey to Brindisi was endured with stops "for food – at one place we had macaroni, calf's brain, beef cheese, chives and Capri wine."

The night cold was kept at bay by "foot warmers which they changed every few hours," and the landscape was a constant attraction:

After we left Bologna and it was light enough we could see the Adriatic Sea on our left hand. Sometimes so close that you could throw a stone into it. The scenery was of course quite new and many strange things attracted one's attention. The blue of the sky (though it was dull and cloudy part of the time). Sandy hills, olive trees, vines, mud huts, villas with painted plaster blue or green, no hedges and few trees until we came within two hours of Brindisi, women washing in a stream, oxen drawing carts or ploughing – I saw a team of six – mules, donkeys and dogs which always barked and tried to keep up with the train, men with blue cloaks, women with yellow shawls round their necks.

At Brindisi there was a pause, and then "tomorrow at 2pm we sail for Alexandria in the Austrian Lloyd boat *Cleopatra*." They were well on their way, but these letters underline the demands made on the long-distance tourist in preaviation days. From London, Cairo and the comfort of a bed at Shepheard's Hotel were ten days away.

The inspiration behind the trip, at least for Ferdy, had been Amelia Edwards's best-selling travelogue *A Thousand Miles Up the Nile*. For Edwards and thousands of other well-heeled European travelers, Shepheard's was the first stop. But unlike most of his fellow travelers, Ferdy showed more than a passing interest in the civilization of the pharaohs. During his first week in Cairo he visited the Egyptian Museum four times, marveling at the antiquities while despairing at the conditions in which they were stored (plus ça change). On arriving at Giza, like many a tourist at the time, he climbed to the top of the Great Pyramid to take in the view, before taking tea on the veranda of the Mena House Hotel—where his fellow guests included Arthur Conan Doyle.

The journey upstream was no less eventful. Ferdy's boat was blown against rocks and ran aground on numerous sandbanks. The river was busy with tourist traffic, and one day Ferdy "passed the Duke of Cambridge in a Khedival steam dahabeeah [*dahabiya*] flying the Royal Standard."

Flinders Petrie

Although lacking any formal education, British Egyptologist Flinders Petrie (1853–1942) learned surveying from his father and brought a new, scientific approach to the discipline of archaeology. He first visited Egypt in 1880 to make a survey of the Giza Pyramids, and went on to excavate at nearly every site of significance during a career spanning over forty years. He made more major discoveries than any other archaeologist in Egypt, and in 1892 was appointed to the first chair in Egyptology in England, at University College London. He published around one thousand books and articles, and is widely regarded as one of the greatest Egyptologists of all time.

In Luxor Ferdy met Egyptological royalty in the person of Flinders Petrie, the "father of Egyptian archaeology." Ferdy wrote to his brother Erny:

I have enjoyed this trip immensely. We spent three days here on the way up (vide timetable) and the day before I left I spent over at the Ramesseum with Prof. Flinders Petrie who invited me to lunch, tea and dinner. I saw a great many things of interest. Petrie, his colleague Mr Guibel. Miss Guibel, Miss Pirie and Miss Paget live together in a house which is about three thousand years old, as it is one of the great granaries or store chambers of the Ramesseum. I saw Petrie take out the foundation deposit of a temple of Amenhotep II (BC 1400) consisting of the bones of the ox which was sacrificed, earthen vessels which contain resin, leaves of fruit or their remains (the ants had eaten most of them), bronze nails etc. I also saw mummy pets packed and he gave me two of the many small figures which were buried with the mummy. I came back across the river to the steamer by moonlight after a most interesting day.

Although the entertainment provided by Petrie may not have been as glamorous as it sounds—his lifestyle was notoriously ascetic—there is no doubt that Ferdy would only have been welcomed into the circle if his Egyptological credentials were entirely acceptable. In his element, Ferdy sought out the tombs and temples on the west bank of Thebes—while his traveling companion bagged quail. At Luxor Ferdy was also excited to meet "two ladies who went up the Nile with Amelia Edwards."

Ferdy was elated by his first visit to Egypt, although by the time he had got to Naples on his return journey he was writing to his mother that "I begin to long for good English beef, tea, tobacco and whiskey." He also wrote to his brother that "I never saw a plainer set of women than in Naples which is rather a surprise. Priests and monks abound."

What Ferdy could not have foreseen was that ten years later he would be returning to the Nile in the company of the family and friends of one of the preeminent grandees and statesmen of his time. It would be a demanding experience, but one which would widen his knowledge not only of Egyptology and its most prominent contemporary players but also of the stratified society in which he was locked. He would then be writing not to his mother but to his wife. Toward the end of his first visit there is a hint of the changes to come. On his return to London he would be staying first, he told his mother, with Mrs. West—soon to become his mother-in-law.

The duke and his party

Spencer Compton Cavendish, the 8th Duke of Devonshire, was one of the most important politicians of the late nineteenth century, and was often called the last of the Whigs, "a body of public men who were in politics not out of zealotry or ambition but from a sense of tradition which is rational, cultivated, respectful of differences and public-spirited."[4] He also stood at the very end of a social era, when the great London houses and their aristocratic owners wielded significant power and influence.

During his political career the duke had for five years been leader of the Liberal Party and had served in three cabinets, refusing three times to be prime minister. He was almost the last head of one of the great families of England to fill the public role dictated by his birth.

The duke's private life, however, most particularly during his earlier years as Lord Hartington (and as such nicknamed "Harty Tarty" by the Prince of Wales), was unconventional. He did not marry until very late in life, and only when he was finally free to marry his longtime mistress, Louise, Duchess of Manchester. Before Louise, Hartington had had an affair from 1859 to 1862 with the famous society courtesan Catherine Walters, known as "Skittles," for whom he would provide support until the end of his life. After Skittles, however, he was faithful, for the next thirty years, to his Duchess of Manchester.

When the evidently compliant Duke of Manchester died in 1890, everyone expected Louise to marry Hartington after a reasonable lapse of time. However, Hartington's father the 7th Duke of Devonshire was himself close to death, which was to occur in December 1891. It was therefore not until August 1892 that the new duke and his lover, now sixty years of age, were married in a private ceremony in London. Louise, originally a von Alten from the oldest nobility of Hanover, was henceforth known as the "Double Duchess." Before her marriage to the political 8th Duke of Devonshire, as he now was, Louise was already established as one of the legendary beauties of high society and a prominent political hostess. After it she became the leading political and society hostess of her age, and was said to be the most powerful person outside the government. Her renowned house parties at Chatsworth were attended by the Prince and Princess of Wales (the future King Edward VII and Queen Alexandra) and epitomized the fashionable country-house life of the epoch.

One can only guess at how much of this gilded social scene would have been familiar to Ferdy, but as a well-informed Londoner, he was probably broadly aware of the antics of its leading players. However, the elderly and quite decrepit couple who were subsequently to be his employers for the Nile journey were certainly by then a shadow of their former fashionable selves. Earlier in the year that Ferdy's trip commenced, the duke had made what was to be his last speech in the House of Lords in June 1907. On June 5, the duke and duchess had held their usual Derby Day dinner and dance, and in mid-June they went to Windsor for Ascot Week. The duke was, however, taken ill and was unable to attend the races. He was taken back to London "suffering from acute heart weakness complicated with a considerable settlement of water on the lungs."[5] After summering at Compton Place, their country house near London, the Devonshires set out on October 24 to winter in Egypt.

Their principal companions for the trip on the Nile were the Earl and Countess of Gosford, who had of course accompanied the duke on his 1890 visit to Egypt, on that occasion with all their children. In 1907 they had only one of their three daughters, Lady Theodosia Acheson, with them.

Louisa Gosford was the second daughter of the duchess by her first husband, the Duke of Manchester, and in 1876 she had married the Earl of Gosford, a sporting Irish landowner with a large castle and a tendency for a "fast" lifestyle. He was a leading member of the Prince of Wales's set, and both the Gosfords at times held Royal Household appointments to the Prince and Princess of Wales.

Lady Theodosia, or "Theo," whom Ferdy was to find aloof, was in a later era to become a political hostess in her own right—by which time she had already been immortalized by John Singer Sargent, whose famous society portrait of the three Acheson sisters hangs at Chatsworth to this day. She was in fact later known for her charm and it appears that there may have been an explanation for her apparent moodiness. There is a society picture of her on the cover of *The Bystander* of January 15, 1908—a date early on in the Nile journey—as having just announced her engagement to the Hon. Thomas Agar-Robartes, son of Lord Clifden, captioned "who was unseated from [his parliamentary seat of] Bodmin owing to a technical breach of the Corruption Act." It would seem odd to depart on a four-month journey immediately after such an apparently happy announcement. Ferdy makes no reference to an engagement and the marriage never took place.

The sixth member of the duke's party, Sir Charles Cradock-Hartopp appears at first a conundrum, as a divorced single man of no apparent distinction (and according to the baronetage of the day, only two thousand acres to his name). However Henry Vane, in his *Affair of State: A Biography of the 8th Duke and Duchess of Devonshire*, does much to explain his presence:

> The Devonshire House circle exhibited the capriciousness of Edwardian social inclusion noted by G.K. Chesterton in *The Queer Feet*. People were mysteriously in without necessarily being aristocratic or rich or brilliant. The duke on his side refused to bow to certain social rules. One of his younger friends was Sir Charles Hartopp, 5th Baronet, whose wife was a Wilson of the Tranby Croft family, and they stayed at Chatsworth several times. But in December 1902 Lady Hartopp sued her husband for divorce on the grounds of adultery. The duke agreed to appear as a witness for Hartopp – who simply hoped thereby to impress the jury – and when the divorce was granted refused to drop him as convention demanded, continuing to invite him to stay. The court appearance provided a touch that amused Max Beerbohm, who much appreciated Devonshire ("my favourite Duke, the most natural and monumental"); he cited the following exchange from the report:
>
>> Counsel: "I think it is a fact, Your Grace, that the petitioner and the respondent and the co-respondent were among the party of guests entertained by you and the Duchess at Chatsworth House last year from January 12th to January 17th."
>> The Witness: "What!" [6]

Sir Charles was a man about town, caricatured by *Vanity Fair* as "Topps," but he was the one passenger with whom Ferdy felt some rapport. But then Sir Charles and Ferdy had in common the fact that neither of them was an aristocrat.

Ferdy Platt and his family

Ferdy Platt was inevitably the outsider: present by reason of his professional expertise, socially acceptable at the dinner table, the most academically cultured of those present, and yet clearly not entirely comfortable in their midst.

The Rowley in Ferdy's full name was important to his family, having been attached through several generations—his father had been Charles Rowley and Ferdy's son was christened simply Rowley. As the senior male of his line of the Platt family, Ferdy possessed a charming full-length portrait of an Anne Rowley of Lower Court, Lugwardine, in the English county of Herefordshire, at the time a girl of about twelve years, her dates 1750–1828 inscribed on the canvas. Ferdy also had a 1790s portrait of the heir to Anne's estate, whose daughter had married Samuel Platt, Ferdy's grandfather—and two of his own father, one painted when he first entered Eton as a scholar in the 1830s and the other when he was commissioned as an Ensign in the 60th Foot[7] in 1842, dressed in the uniform of the Napoleonic Wars. With the portraits Ferdy had inherited some fine eighteenth-century furniture and other trappings of gentility.

Ferdy therefore was both "landed gentry" and "military" by background, both important indicators of Victorian and Edwardian social status. His patrimonial Platt lineage was itself modestly distinguished—predominantly a succession of successful London barristers stretching back to the mid-eighteenth century, and including Sir Thomas Joshua Platt, who had been knighted as Baron of the Exchequer[8] in 1843. Earlier Platts had included a Fellow of the Royal Society,[9] while Ferdy's grandfather, Samuel Platt, with a house in London's Russell Square, had been a deputy lieutenant of Middlesex,[10] suggesting an established and prosperous position in London society.

Sadly, the Herefordshire estate and the fruits of a century of lawyering had over the generations been frittered or even, it was rumored, gambled away. Samuel had sent his four sons to Eton and then into the army, valuable in the context of Victorian social acceptability but not conducive to the prosperity of future generations. The military tradition would last for another hundred years but, fortunately for the readers of his letters, bypass Ferdy. His father, ultimately Colonel Charles Rowley Platt, was as a result of intervention by the Duke of Cambridge,[11] appointed in 1886 a Military Knight of Windsor[12] by Queen Victoria, who considered him "a fit object for our royal charity." Ferdy's parents were therefore given chambers in Windsor Castle above Henry VIII's Gate, where they ended their days and which Ferdy, at the time of his first letters from Egypt in 1896, would have referred to as "home." Ferdy's brother Ernest ("Erny"), whom we encounter in the letters as being short of funds, would end his days as a retired Colonel in Cheltenham.

Ferdy's father had evidently had enough money earlier in his career to provide for his eldest son to follow him to Eton—or maybe the formerly prosperous grandfather Samuel paid the fees. At all events Ferdy, as his later firm grasp of Egyptology would suggest, repaid his privileged education with a serious

approach to his studies. These took him subsequently to Edinburgh University
then acknowledged as the national center for the study of medicine, and in due
course on to his professional career as a London physician.

Ferdy had also had sufficient resources to make his first trip up the Nile
in 1896, although there are perhaps telling references to the generosity o
his companion Reiss. In the ten years between that first visit and his voyage
accompanying the Duke of Devonshire, Ferdy had made a propitious move
He had met and married Mabel or "May" West, a cultured lady from a well-
to-do family in St. John's Wood in North London. May brought with her some
financial security, which may explain Ferdy's later apparently relaxed approach
to the economic challenges of life. Egyptology was his passion and the Nile trip
with the duke was evidently to be the great adventure of his life. Later pictures
show him to be an apparently benign and fulfilled family man.

Ferdy's letters provide ample evidence of his close affection for his two
children, born to May in the early years of the twentieth century. Violet was to
be the beloved recipient of his Egyptian box and Rowley, his son and heir.

Within the fine gradations of Edwardian society, Ferdy would be placed most
probably in the "metropolitan upper middle class." It was likely to have been the
metropolitan characteristic and his "cultured" nature which resulted in his remaining at some social distance from his fellow passengers, and at times sensitive to
hints of condescension—although certainly not from the courteous duke.

Notes

1 A.H.Sayce, *Reminiscences* (London: Macmillan, 1923), 211.
2 Sayce, *Reminiscences*, 175.
3 Now the Egypt Exploration Society.
4 Henry Vane, *Affair of State: A Biography of the 8th Duke and Duchess o
   Devonshire* (London: Peter Owen, 2004), 248.
5 Vane, *Affair of State*, 246.
6 Vane, *Affair of State*, 239–40.
7 A designation for the King's Royal Rifle Corps, a regiment of the British Army
   that served for two hundred years throughout the Empire but has since disappeared following successive regimental amalgamations.
8 A senior judicial appointment of great antiquity. Dissolved in 1880, the Exchequer of Pleas or Court of Exchequer dealt with matters of equity. Sir Thomas
   Joshua Platt KC (1788–1862) was appointed a Baron of the Exchequer in
   1848.
9 The national science academy of the United Kingdom, and the oldest scientific
   academy in continuous existence, having first met in 1600 following a lecture
   by Sir Christopher Wren.

10 A ceremonial office, appointed by the lord lieutenant to assist him or her in official duties. The lord lieutenant is the monarch's representative in each county, charged with upholding the dignity of the crown. Samuel Platt was a deputy lieutenant for the county of Middlesex, now subsumed into Greater London.

11 Prince George, Duke of Cambridge (1850–1904), grandson of King George III. He had no heirs and the title died with him, to be recreated for Prince William in 2011.

12 The Military Knights of Windsor are retired military officers who receive a pension and accommodation in the precincts of Windsor Castle. In return, they provide ceremonial support at services in St. George's Chapel Windsor, notably the annual service for the Order of the Garter. They were constituted by King Edward III following the Battle of Crécy (1346) when many knights captured by the French were forced to liquidate their estates to raise ransom.

3

Ferdy's Letters Home to London

Upstream from Cairo

A fter traveling by train and steamer from England via France and Italy to Alexandria and thence to Cairo, Ferdy and the other members of the Duke of Devonshire's party joined their Nile boat, the SS *Serapis*, at Bulaq, the port of Cairo, on Thursday, November 7, 1907. All around them boats were being made ready for the start of the winter cruising season up the Nile. Later that afternoon, the *Serapis* weighed anchor and its passengers and crew began their voyage upstream. As they journeyed south, against the river's current, they sailed at a leisurely pace, stopping frequently to visit the major archaeological sites en route.

The first attraction on the itinerary was the ancient necropolis of Saqqara, still in its early days of excavation. Here, Ferdy met James Quibell, the first of many eminent archaeologists he was to encounter during his Nile journey. Less than a week later, the *Serapis* moored at el-Hagg Qandil, and Ferdy was able to visit the ruins of Amarna, the short-lived capital city of the heretic pharaoh Akhenaten. First excavated by the great Flinders Petrie at the end of the nineteenth century, Amarna was still to yield up its greatest treasure, the painted bust of Nefertiti, which a German expedition would find five years after Ferdy's visit.

In the following days, brief stops were made at Asyut, Abydos (to view the magnificent temple of Seti I), and Dendera, before the *Serapis* reached Luxor on Friday, November 22, fifteen days after leaving Cairo. During the next ten days, Ferdy immersed himself in the glories of ancient Thebes, visiting the great temple of Karnak by moonlight, the immense edifice of Medinet Habu, and the Valley of the Kings, still in mid-excavation. His guides to pharaonic treasures included Arthur Weigall and Edward Ayrton, both at the prime of their archaeological careers.

Continuing southward, along that most picturesque of stretches of the Nile that runs between Luxor and Cairo, Ferdy visited marvels of engineering ancient and modern, ranging from the temple of Horus at Edfu and the sandstone quarries of Gebel al-Silsila to the Esna barrage and the irrigation works at Kom Ombo. His guide at the last site was none other than Sir William Willcocks, perhaps the most celebrated hydraulic engineer of the Edwardian era.

On Sunday, December 8, a month and a day after setting out from Cairo, the *Serapis* arrived at Aswan, pearl of Upper Egypt, for a three-week sojourn. Perhaps nowhere else in Egypt enjoys such a splendid winter climate as Aswan, and the ailing duke took full advantage of the restorative warmth and sunshine. This extended stay afforded Ferdy ample opportunity to visit the key sites of Aswan and Elephantine, and to meet two of the greatest Egyptologists of the day, the American George Andrew Reisner and the Englishman Alan Gardiner. While moored at Aswan, the duke's party celebrated Christmas 1907—a bittersweet experience for the increasingly homesick Ferdy. Altogether more memorable was an encounter, on their final day in Aswan, with the young Winston Churchill on his way back down the Nile from Uganda—a historic meeting, indeed.

Just four days' sailing beyond Aswan, with a short stop on New Year's Day 1908 to view the rock-cut temples at Abu Simbel, brought Ferdy and his companions to Wadi Halfa, a town at the foot of the Second Nile Cataract, and the southernmost stop on the classic Nile cruise. This marked the turning point in their voyage—a chance to send and receive mail, take a donkey ride to the rock of Abusir to look down upon the Cataract, and make preparations for the return trip downstream.

Ferdy's letters to his wife were informal and his spelling, some of it archaic ("staid" rather than "stayed"), has been retained. He appeared to prefer to refer to his son Rowley as "Rowly," and so forth.

SS *Serapis* anchored at Bedreshein 15 miles from Cairo
6.30 pm Thursday Nov. 7 1907

My dearest May,

We left our moorings this afternoon beside the *Rameses*[1] at 2.45 and although I finished a letter and posted it before we started I am beginning another this evening so as to keep abreast of events. The Gosfords and Sir C.H. went into Cairo this morning but I did not feel inclined so stayed on board. Lady Theo also as she was ill – I saw her after breakfast and again this evening. She [ate] something which disagreed with her. The *Rameses* "next door" was being got ready to start next Tuesday and the men were cleaning the deck. Natives with bare feet. Each man had a bundle of some sort of twigs under his right foot. The deck was wet and sprinkled with sand or holystone. One man in front began to sing a few words and then the rest joined in chorus. As they did so each man worked his right foot up along the deck then brought his left nearer to his right then right foot down – in this way they gradually moved along the deck in unison. I was very glad when we started as we were quite shut in all round with canvas which not only kept off the sun and prevented people looking in but it kept out the wind and prevented me getting any view and what is worse kept in the mosquitoes and midges. We have been horribly bitten and the irritation is disagreeable everyone is scratching and putting on all sorts of things.

This afternoon we started in rather cloudy weather but with a pleasant cool north wind. A few days ago it was south and hot. We are anchored at Bedreshein which is opposite to Helwan and to the left of the latter (ie to the North) are the quarries of Turra [Tura] and Masarah, where the Anc. Eg. [Ancient Egyptians] got the best quality of lime stone.[2] I visited them with Reiss[3] and had lunch in one of them. I bought a thermometer in Cairo and have hung it in my cabin temp tonight (7 o'clock) 69°F. I have been hunting mosquitoes and killing several.

---

1   Another passenger boat, the one in which Ferdy traveled up the Nile in 1896 (see letter of November 15).
2   The fine white limestone from the Tura quarries was used for the casing blocks of many Old Kingdom pyramids, and for many of the finest temple buildings and reliefs.
3   His companion on his 1896 trip.

On board the *Serapis*, Bedreshein
Friday Nov. 8th 1907 6pm

We have just returned from our trip to Sakkara.[1] "We" means Lord and Lady G. and myself. Mr Quibell[2] came to the boat this morning 8.30 and we left about 9.15 with him riding on donkeys a short distance to the village of Bedreshein among palm trees, then we had a delightful sail in a native boat over the inundated country to the edge of the desert. From there we went on donkeys to see Quibell's excavations going on, in a Coptic monastery[3] which dates back to at least 800 AD and possibly 600 AD and in which there are columns with fine capitals. There are also many paintings of saints and apostles which although very rough, crude and bad art are interesting. Then we went to see some work he was doing at the Step Pyramid[4] where some of the casing was visible also the wall which surrounded the Pyramid. Then the tomb of Ptah-hetep[5] which is very fine especially the painted sculptures showing the trades etc. We then had lunch in Mariette's[6] old house, after which we saw the tomb of Tii,[7] and a new tomb which he has just discovered. All these belong to the Old Empire[8] V Dyn[asty] or VI Dyn[asty] somewhere about 3000 BC.[9] In

---

1   Archaeological site on the west bank of the Nile, part of the necropolis of the ancient capital city of Memphis. It has perhaps the greatest concentration of funerary monuments anywhere in Egypt, spanning the entire sweep of ancient Egyptian history from the First Dynasty to the Christian period.

2   James Edward Quibell (1867–1935), British Egyptologist. In 1905, he was appointed chief inspector of antiquities at Saqqara, excavating sites with the assistance of his wife Annie.

3   The Monastery of Apa Jeremias.

4   The earliest pyramid in Egypt, built for king Djoser at the beginning of the Third Dynasty (c. 2650 BC). Quibell, assisted by Cecil Firth, would go on to conduct the first systematic excavation of the Step Pyramid and its complex of buildings.

5   A high official of the Fifth Dynasty (c. 2350 BC), who served as vizier and an overseer of royal pyramid complexes.

6   François Auguste Ferdinand Mariette (1821–1881), French Egyptologist and founder of the Egyptian Antiquities Service.

7   A high official of the Fifth Dynasty (c. 2400 BC), who served as an overseer of royal pyramid complexes and sun temples, as well as a royal hairdresser.

8   Now called the Old Kingdom.

9   In the decades following Ferdy's visit, scholarship steadily lowered the dates of the Old Kingdom and earlier periods of ancient Egyptian history. The Fifth and Sixth Dynasties are now dated to c. 2450–2325 BC and c. 2325–2175 BC, respectively.

the last tomb there had been a later burial and Lady G. took away a piece of a lower jaw with 3 teeth for the Duchess and when we got back I was asked to extract one of the teeth in order that the D might carry it in her purse for luck!

After seeing these tombs we went to Quibell's house and had tea. He has the most magnificent views from the veranda and windows and still finer views from the upper story rooms as the house is built on the high desert plateau and commands the Nile Valley from Cairo and the Pyramids in the north to Helwan and the eastern hills opposite, the inundation, and Dashour on the south. After tea he accompanied us on our donkey ride back to the boat and said good bye. The sun set just before we landed and the donkey ride to the *Serapis* was concluded just as it became dark. There was and still is a strong wind blowing and while we were in the boat a few drops of rain fell. The sunset was fine. It was an interesting day. I am now going to rest before dinner. Tell the children that I saw such [a] dear little pussie at Quibels house blue grey with such long legs and so affectionate.

On board the *Serapis* anchored near Rigga or Rikka
6.30 pm Nov. 9th 1907 Saturday

We left Bedreschein this morning soon after 11 with a strong cold north wind blowing which necessitated an overcoat until after lunch. Great clouds of sand were being blown along the desert and often on the sand banks there were small clouds of sand while the Nile was just like the sea with white crested waves. We passed number of herons fishing on the edge of the sand banks and dozens of shadufs[1] at work, although the Nile is high but it has been a bad Nile not high enough this year so the shadufs have got to work early. There has been a good deal of cloud since I came to Egypt but today the sky was quite clear. The cold wind lowered the temp. in my room to 65°F last night and diminished the number of

---

1   Irrigation device used for lifting water from the river or a canal on to fields. The *shaduf* comprises a long horizontal pole with a bucket at one end and a counterweight at the other, mounted on a vertical stake.

mosquitoes I am thankful to say. Everyone has been bitten except Lord Gosford. My face is a sight but not so bad as Lady G.'s maid who looked as if she had smallpox. My hands arms and ankles also have been attacked. The Duchess had about twenty marks or more on each arm. They itch like fury especially at night. I have tried all kinds of things but nothing seems to do much good except scratching and then putting on resinol. I tried ammonia, carbolic acid, ether, etc. but nothing seems much use.

No sightseeing today but I had a little surgery to do. I had just sat down to lunch with the rest and had begun the second course when our Dragoman Selim came and asked me to see the engineer who had met with an accident. The glass tube of the water gauge burst and cut his face and nose just below his eye. I had to put two stitches in. The next excitement was that my cabin was flooded. I had a regular inundation. I wanted some water to wash my hands before I dressed the engineer's wound but I could not get any from my tap. I thought the tank was empty so I ran down to attend to him. When I came up and went back to lunch water began to run into the basin and flooded the floor of my cabin. However no harm was done only my slippers got wet. We have a dragoman – who manages everything, orders the dinner and writes the menu in his best French! – a reis or captain of the ship, a steersman, several sailors and several waiters. The Dragoman is Syrian (most of them are). The engineer is Italian; the rest, native Egyptians. After dark the electric light is turned on and the dynamo makes a good deal of row and vibration; in fact I can't imagine how they can sit in the smoking room and play "Bridge" where they are just over it, as the vibration there is very bad – in fact you might just as well be in a motor bus.

Not so far from where we are is the Pyramid of Mêdum which is older than the Great Pyramid having been built by the king who preceded Khufu.[1] You will see a photo of it in my big album. The Duke's man looks after my things and did all my packing at Mena House[2] which is a great relief to me.

---

1   The pyramid of Medum was completed by the Fourth Dynasty King Sneferu (c. 2575 BC), Khufu's father and predecessor.
2   Once a royal hunting lodge, the Mena House opened as a hotel in 1886, catering to tourists visiting the Pyramids.

Benisuef – 172 miles from Cairo[1]
Nov. 10th Sunday

Went for a walk before breakfast with Sir C. Hartopp. Walked along a
bank and saw them irrigating the fields, saw a hoopoe,[2] Ba-lambs, moo
cows and donkeys. Lord G., Sir C. and I get up about 6.30 and have tea on
deck. It is the nicest time of the day. We went with Sir C. for a short sail in
his boat which is called the Ibis. We left our moorings at 11.30 am exactly
and steamed all day. We had several fine views of the Pyramids of Medum.
I examined the Duke last night: he is very much better; his cough is much
less and expectoration less but he still goes to sleep very easily. Lady G. has
been seedy all day and I had to see her and prescribe. She told me that I
am the only Doctor the Duke has had any confidence in. He believes most
doctors are humbugs. She complimented me upon the way I had managed
him. We arrived here off Benisuef about sunset and had the ship made fast
off an island between us and the town. L.G., Lady T., Sir C. and self walked
across it till we came to the small channel separating us from the town then
walked back; the island is about a mile across and several long. I am going
to post this tomorrow morning before we start if possible.

I am looking forward to your next letter darling. As I go farther away from
Cairo I shall have to await longer for your letters. The express post boats
will of course catch us up but there must be some delay. Lots of shadufs,
Indian corn 8 or ten feet high.

No time for more. Much love darling to you and the chicks. I hope Violet
is getting on with her reading and writing.

Your loving husband
A.F.R. Platt

---

1   This is an error: Benisuef is 72 miles from Cairo (see Ferdy's letter of November 12).
2   Colorful crested bird, found throughout the Mediterranean lands, and a common sight in
    Egypt.

On board *Serapis* between <u>Kolosseneh</u> (or <u>Kulusana</u>) and <u>Minieh</u> [Minya] about 140 miles from Cairo

Tuesday Nov. 12th 1907

My dearest May,

I was unable to post the letter after all yesterday as no one went into the town. As it will not go till we get to Minieh I have opened it and am adding a few lines. I believe we shall receive our letters tomorrow at Minieh as the dragoman will telegraph for them as soon as he lands to be sent on there so we shall get them in the morning, in which case I hope to have one from you and to add a line after I have read it. There was nothing much to record yesterday. We left Benisuef (73 miles from Cairo) at 9.25 am and anchored for the night on the W. bank opposite to Sharoua. Lady G. was better but I managed to get tummy ache and diarrhoea but it did not last long and I am right again. We left Sharoua about 8.45 this morning. It is very warm and comfortable. Last night it was chilly. My thermometer has been down to 58°F. Just now (1 o'clock) it is 69°F. Lunch ready.

2.40 pm – we are not far from Minieh now. The scenery has been more interesting today. The lime stone cliffs coming down close to the river. We passed a quarry just as they fired a blasting charge and saw the stone come tumbling down. Tell Violet and Boy that a dear little wag tail flew on board and walked up and down the deck picking up crumbs. He was so tame . . . grey with black markings with a white face and breast and black beak and legs. Such thin legs and beak. Lord G. put out some bread for him but his beak was too small to manage anything but the crumbs. Yesterday was washing day and this morning all the things were hanging up to dry round the rails and posts on the fore part of the deck. This morning we saw on the bank a thing which looked like a small bee hive on four legs with four handles: it was a coffin! Waiting to be taken across to the cemetery on the other side of the Nile.

We are close to Minieh now and I must post this as soon as we get there as there may be no time tomorrow morning to write after I get your letter, so good bye darling. I hope Violet's nettle rash is better and that you are all well and happy. Have you a new maid yet?

Much love darling from your affectionate husband
A.F.R. Platt

On board the *Serapis* anchored off Gebel Abu Feda north of Manfalut
10 pm Thursday Nov. 14th 1907

My darling,

I have been reading through your letter again dated Oct 29–30th as I did not get one at Minieh as I expected although the Duke did. I hope to get one tomorrow at Assyut when we arrive there. I have only received two letters so far. One I found at Cook's[1] on arriving at Cairo and one came to the boat before we left Cairo.

We left Minieh yesterday morning at 9.30 am. At 12.30 we reached Benihassan where there are the well known XII Dyn. tombs but we did not stop there much to the disappointment of all the donkey boys who began to collect as soon as our steamer was in sight. I was not sorry as I have been there before[2] and the tombs are so damaged that it [is] difficult to make much out on the walls. We steamed on till we came to Hagg Kandeel where we staid the night. You never sail at night on the Nile.

After we arrived at Minieh Sir C. and I went for a walk up the main street of the town as far as the railway station. Walking behind us was one of our sailors, as they always send some one with you when you land. On our way back we met the Duke, the Duchess and Lady Theo – attended by two or three men from the boat, our dragoman and native policemen and a staring rear guard of small children. The Duchess was dressed in white

---

1   The office of Thomas Cook & Son, located inside the old Shepheard's Hotel in Cairo.
2   On Ferdy's earlier visit in 1896.

flannel with a big bunch of artificial violets or something and a white flat hat. She has a beautiful colour on each cheek. It was rather amusing to see all this in the midst of such a thoroughly oriental setting.

Hagg Kandeel is the landing place from which you visit the tombs of Tel el Amarna[1] and the painted pavement in the ruins of the palace of Akh en Aten or Khu en Aten as he used to be called.[2] The heretic king who worshipped the sun's disc. I got up at 6 am bathed shaved had breakfast and left on a donkey at 7.15 for some of the tombs about an hour's donkey ride. On the way back I saw the painted pavement which was discovered by Petrie[3] and is under cover. The tombs were much damaged but the pavement is interesting. When I returned I changed my things (knickers and Norfolk[4]) and had a wash. The Duke, Lord Gosford, Lady Theo and Sir C. then started off to see the pavement and I went again, as it was the Duke's first excursion. He was carried in a chair with poles by the men. Although the dragoman went I was the real guide. The Duke was none the worse for his outing and made the best meal (at lunch) since he came to Egypt.

9.15 am Friday Nov. 15th 1907

We left our anchorage at 8.15 am and are now on our way to Assiut which we ought to reach about 2 pm. I hope to find a letter from you when we get there. There is so much that I want to write about but I find it difficult to get it all in and think of it. At sunset yesterday we [were] going to anchor close under the great lime stone cliffs of Gebel Abu Fêda where there is a gap in the rock and a sandy bottom close to a Coptic cemetery

1   Archaeological site on the east bank of the Nile where Akhenaten founded his new capital city.

2   Akhenaten, tenth king of the Eighteenth Dynasty (reigned c. 1353–36 BC).

3   Petrie uncovered the painted pavement in the ruins of a royal palace during his excavations at Amarna in 1891–92.

4   Norfolk jacket: a loose, belted, single-breasted jacket very popular in the Edwardian era, made fashionable by the Prince of Wales (later King Edward VII), whose country residence (Sandringham) was in Norfolk. The Norfolk jacket was originally designed as a shooting coat that did not bind when the elbow was raised to fire.

and a disused Coptic monastery built in the ancient quarry, but her Grace is superstitious and we had to move on.

I wish I could describe Gebel Abu Feda properly. It is a very fine stretch of cliff extending several miles close to the water, full of quarries and small holes cut in the rock here and there in groups for mummied cats, jackals, etc. Tell Violet and Boy that I saw 15 pelicans swimming down past our steamer early this morning and we see lots of camels!!

I have my bath at 7 o'clock. Generally I am up at 6.30. It is odd that one feels one must get up as soon as it gets light. The morning is the best time of day. I don't know how long this early rising will last, but L.G., Sir C. and I are always up about that time. I have my breakfast at 8.30; the rest have theirs in driblets later. If I did not have my bath before 7.30 there would be no chance of getting it till very late and I like to have my breakfast while it is cool in the dining room. We are just passing the openings of tombs at Ma'abda opposite Manfalut where the crocodile mummies were buried.[1] Just before we started this morning the "*Rameses*" came up (the boat I went up in 11 years ago). It brought two suits of clothes for Sir C. made in Cairo and supplied us with ice, which we had run short of. On board is the engineer (Graham) who went inside the Gt. Pyramid with me. Being early there were very few on deck but his little girl was looking out of her cabin and waved to us. They went on a quarter of an hour before we did, so we follow on and see their funnel mast and smoke across the bends of the river. Not so many mosquitoes now. But I always have a hunt in my cabin before dressing for dinner. By the way dinner jacket and black tie still worn!

I shall post this at Assyut but not today probably as I believe we are going to stay a couple of days. It is a big place, the largest town in upper Egypt. Fine bazaar. Tombs at the back. We are now about 225 miles from Cairo. I am writing this on deck. It is difficult to write in my cabin and the smoking room is used as a sitting room (where you mustn't smoke on account of the Duke) and one can only get in to write before breakfast. The dining room can't be used till after the dinner things have been removed as the cloth is

---

1   A catacomb of mummified crocodiles and other animals situated on the east bank of the Nile, about 5 km northeast of the village of al-Maabda. Baedeker's guide described it as "hardly worth visiting, as practically nothing is to be seen except the charred remains of the mummies of crocodiles." None the less, Flaubert visited during his travels in Egypt in 1849, returning to France with a mummified human foot which he kept in his study as he wrote *Madame Bovary*. The 'crocodile cave' thus acquired a certain notoriety among late Victorian and Edwardian travelers.

laid all day. The days pass quickly as there is always something to look at and people talk to me and ask me all sorts of questions about all sorts of things.

Lord G. is an extremely nice man and full of dry quiet humour. Sir C.H. is pleasant but cares for little but sport, and things Egyptological bore him. They both give me cigars now and then and are friendly. Lady G. likes to discuss literature and "science generally" with me but not before the Duchess. I speak less to her than anyone else as she seems to talk more about people than ideas, although I think she knows a good deal. She is old and infirm and talks rather sparingly. She, the Duke, Lady G. and Sir C. play bridge after tea to dinner and after dinner to bed time. Lord G. hates being expected to play any day so does not play at all. Lady Theo is quite young and rather distant but talks to me more than she did. She does not seem to have much in her, but at meals she says so little except common place things that I can't judge; as you know I am rather deaf or at least I say "what" a good many times. Well it would drive you frantic here no one ever asks a question or makes a remark to some one else without some one saying "<u>what</u>". The fact is, with the exception of the Duke, no one speaks distinctly. Sir C.H. is given to speakin' and huntin' and "if I was you". Lady G. speaks fairly well but is not very sure of some words – "Astromony" for example. I ought to write to several people but find it all I can do to write to you darling. I must try at Assyut. The shaking of the ship by day and the dynamo which works the electric light is rather trying.

We have just arrived at Assyut (2.30 pm Nov. 15 Friday) and I intend to close this letter and post it at once. Thank you darling for your two welcome and long expected letters and paper. I will write again tomorrow only I don't want to miss a mail if there is one. Please put <u>Cairo</u> as well as Egypt as I think there has been some delay.

Your two letters are dated Nov. 3rd and 7th.

Much love darling to you all
Your affect. husband
A.F.R. Platt

xxxxxxxxxx

On board the *Serapis* near Kau el Kebir – 277 miles from Cairo
11 am Sunday Nov. 17th 1907

My darling,

I was unable to get another letter written before leaving Asyut as we left
rather sooner than I expected – about noon the next day and I was unable
to go ashore again to post. I told you we arrived there Friday at 2.30 –
with the exception of Lord G. and myself every one went on shore in the
afternoon. No one went to see the tombs and as it was rather hot, I waited
till the evening and then went for a stroll with Ld. G. and Lady Theo. In
the afternoon I put Kent's camera up and took an experimental photo of
the bank and people on it and a bit of the *Rameses* which was lying near us.
I afterwards went on the *Rameses* and had tea with Mrs Graham, the wife
of the engineer. She had only got up that afternoon as she had been ill
with diarrhoea, which pulled her down very much. So many people seem
to have had it. Yesterday (Saturday) morning at 8 am I drove into Asyut
with Lord G., Lady T. riding on a donkey. We went to the bazars. I tried
to get you a shawl of open network covered with silver, but the dragoman
told me they wanted too much for it. I can't write very well on board as
there is so much vibration from the machinery.

I was so pleased to get your letters dear. Thank you very much for
them also the weekly *Times*.

It seems months since I left home and I begin to wish myself back
again. I should like to pop in suddenly and see what you and the chicks
are doing. I feel rather lonely at times although surrounded by six other
people. By the way there was no one else – no "number 12". Lord Gosford is an extremely nice man, so thoughtful for other people, and as I
told you before full of dry humour. The Duke is a sensible man and his
remarks are generally to the point and so are his questions. He is much
better than he was. Conversation at meals is rather feeble but occasionally
one hears interesting remarks about people in high places.

I don't think I shall see as much as I hoped as the Duke is not up to
much. But I expect I shall be able to do a good deal at Thebes. I think
you would enjoy going up the Nile; there is so much to see for one who

has never been before. The bright sun, blue sky, the limestone cliffs, the shadufs, the women filling and carrying their water jars on their heads, the various birds: storks, herons, pelicans, hawks, vultures, cranes, spoonbills, ducks, geese, etc. At Asyut there were some beautiful Poinsettias and hibiscus. Then the palm trees, Indian corn and sugar cane, the native villages built of Nile mud plastered with white, native boats, camels, donkeys, small goats and sheep, all give variety to the scene. Then there are the sunsets and brilliant stars. Last night a magnificent meteor fell in front of us and seemed to explode into pieces, its reflexion in the water was pretty.

One drawback on this small boat is that one can't get enough exercise . . . I have knocked off a good deal of alcohol and also food in spite of the excellent cook we have. I took the stitches out of the engineer's face this morning. Since I sewed him up I have had several of the crew coming to me for all sorts of things. One man who does the washing wanted me to cut off two fingers as he has six on each hand. I had to get the dragoman to explain that he would be unable to work for several days if I did. I may do it before we leave the boat.

I am very comfortable and enjoying the trip but wish I could get more exercise and smoke a pipe outside my own cabin more than I can. I found Violet's photo in the writing case. I am glad to hear her nettle rash is better. I am very glad too to know that you are seeing plenty of people. I meant to have written to Bottomly but couldn't manage it.

4.45 pm – just arrived Sohag. Going ashore to post this.

Much love darling.

Your loving husband
A.F.R. Platt

On board the *Serapis* anchored off the left bank about 5 miles from Beliana
11 am Wednesday Nov. 20ᵗʰ 1907

My darling,

There are enormous numbers of birds of various kinds: cranes, pelicans, vultures, spoonbills, plover on large sand bank not far from us and, what is more
exciting to Sir Charles and Ld. G., there are hundreds of duck in the water
beyond flying up and floating down stream, so we have moored to the bank
and the rowing boat and Ld. G's "Ibis" are both ready to start off as soon as
there is any wind. And Sir C. hopes to get a shot at some of them. So I am
taking this opportunity now the boat is still of writing a few lines to you.

The paddles go all day and the electric light dynamo starts as soon as the
paddles stop at dusk so we never have any real peace and rest or quiet, except
when the lights go out and the first thing in the morning before we start.
So I am enjoying this stop very much. We went for a short walk at Sohag
just before sunset going through some of the streets. Next day we sailed to
Beliana, which we reached about 3 o'clock and the next morning, that is yesterday, Tuesday 19th, we had breakfast at 8 o'clock and all started off, soon
after 9, on donkeys (except the Duke and Duchess who drove in a carriage
later on) for Abydos, a distance of about 8 miles.

(No chance of getting the duck so we are just off again.)

We saw the temples of Rameses II and Seti I.[1] I was delighted to see the
beautiful sculptured and painted walls in the former once more.[2] We had
lunch in it (Seti's temple).

Lord and Lady G. and the Duke asked me lots of questions and I was kept
busy telling them all about it. Soon after lunch we started off home again. As
this was our first long donkey ride every one was still sore and tired. I went
to bed at 10.30 and slept like a top. The exercise did me a lot of good. Sitting
or standing about all day looking through glasses is not a very healthy way
of passing the time although there is plenty to see. The next place of interest

---

1   Third and second kings of the Nineteenth Dynasty, respectively; reigned c. 1290–1279
     BC (Seti I) and c. 1279–1213 BC (Ramesses II).
2   Ferdy means the earlier of the two temples, that is, that built for King Seti I.

is Dendera[1] – which we shall see the day after tomorrow I think. You might take out my albums and you will be able to picture me at the different places. I have only taken one photo (at Assyut). Lady G. and Lady T. have taken several but they are not very communicative about it. However I am going to ask them for some hints when I get the opportunity. I can do nothing when the boat is moving, of course, with Kent's big camera.

I can't understand why the others get letters more frequently than I do although you post twice a week. I am afraid you will get my letters very irregularly as we only stop at sunset and no one seems to know or care when letters ought to be posted. In fact they are not moved to enthusiasm very much by anything apparently. I intend to post a few lines every day when I can. Sometimes it is not possible as we start early and come home late and sometimes we tie up to the bank far from any railway station or village as I fancy will be the case this evening.

5 pm – Nag Hamadi

It is nearly sunset and I am writing a few lines before posting this. We are close to the Railway Bridge which crosses the Nile at this spot and we can't go on till it opens tomorrow morning at 6 am which we are going to do. We shall get to Denderah about 1.30.

I am now longing to get a letter dearest. It seems ages since I had one and longer still when I see others getting them. I hardly ever see the papers no one offers to lend them and unless I find them lying about I have to wait for the weekly Times. It is nearly a month since I left but it feels more like three. You won't find the Bridge or railway marked on any of my maps: they are all too old but Nag Hamadi is between Beliana and Kena.[2] The hills are just beginning to get pink. There is a long stretch of bank opposite covered with palm trees, then to the left are great bold flat topped cliffs still further to the left is the bank to which we are moored then the masts of a number of native boats then the town of Nag Hamadi which is rather high above the water.

---

1   Archaeological site on the west bank of the Nile, dominated by a well-preserved temple
      of the Ptolemaic and Roman periods, dedicated to the mother-goddess Hathor.
2   The modern spellings are Balyana and Qena, respectively.

The 8th Duke of Devonshire
in Cannes in the 1890s.

Louise, Duchess of
Devonshire, painted
by Edward Hughes
(1832–1908). The
Duchess would only allow
herself to be painted or
photographed in profile.

Chatsworth House, the principal country home of the Devonshires, at the time of the Nile journey.

A shooting party at Chatsworth in 1907. King Edward VII is in the center foreground with the gray-bearded Duke of Devonshire behind his left shoulder. The Duchess, third from left is, as ever, presenting her profile.

The Duke of Devonshire as the Emperor Charles V.

The Duchess of Devonshire as Zenobia, Queen of Palmyra.

The Earl of Gosforth as Robert de la Mark.

Four of the Nile passengers dressed for the costume ball that took place as part of the Queen's Jubilee at the Duke's London home, Devonshire House, in July 1897.

The Countess of Gosforth as Minerva (period of Louis XV).

Ladies Alexandra, Mary, and Theodosia Acheson painted by John Singer Sargent. Almost certainly commissioned by their grandmother the Duchess of Devonshire, and first exhibited at the Royal Academy in 1902.

'Topps' or Sir Charles Cradock-Hartopp, as one of *Vanity Fair*'s Men of the Day in 1912.

This *Bystander* announcement of the engagement of Lady Theodosia occurred as the SS *Serapis* was traveling up the Nile. Evidently no mention was made of it, within Ferdy's hearing, and no marriage took place.

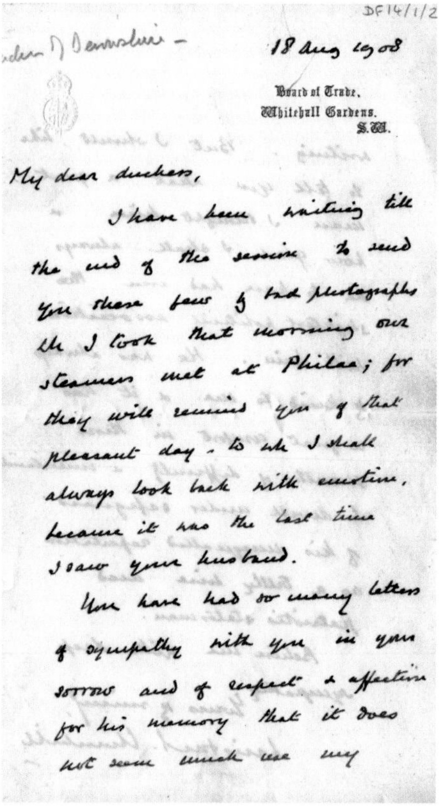

...dss of Devonshire —

18 Aug 1908

Board of Trade,
Whitehall Gardens.
S.W.

My dear duchess,

I have been waiting till the end of the session to send you these few v bad photographs that I took that morning our steamers met at Philae; for they will remind you of that pleasant day — to which I shall always look back with emotion, because it was the last time I saw your husband.

You have had so many letters of sympathy with you in your sorrow and of respect & affection for his memory that it does not seem much use my writing. But I should like to tell you what a great man I thought him & how glad I shall always be to have had even the slightest political association with him. He was always kind to me & it was a great comfort in these months of difficulty & uncertainty to dwell under safeguard of his unequalled reputation as a truly wise and patriotic statesman.

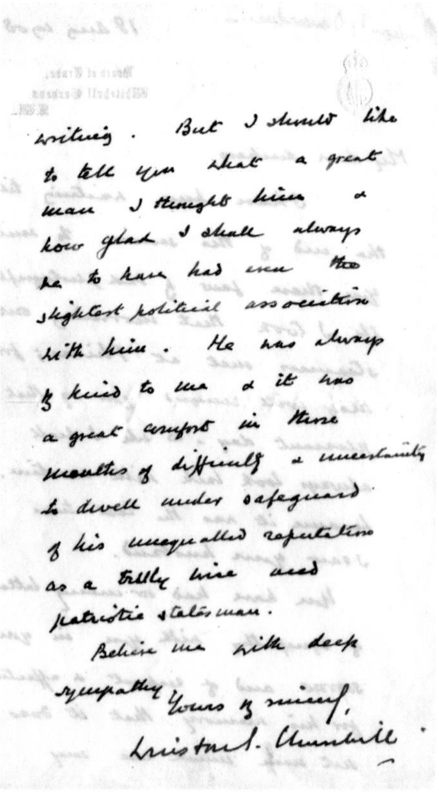

Believe me with deep sympathy Yours sincerely,

Winston S. Churchill

Winston Churchill's letter of condolence to the Duchess written in August 1908, in which he refers to enclosing "these few v bad photographs that I took that morning our steamers met at Philae …"

African Tour. 1908.

1. Sir Edward Marsh.

2. Colonel Gordon Wilson, The Blues.

3. Sir H. Belcher

A page from a Churchill family album of photographs especially taken for the African Tour, and identifying (possibly in the hand of Clementine Churchill) Sir Edward Marsh and Colonel Gordon Wilson.

One of Winston Churchill's "v bad photographs" that did not get sent to the Duchess. It shows the Duke sitting behind the Duchess with possibly a rakish Sir Charles in the foreground, and was recently discovered in the Churchill Archive in Cambridge.

Lady Theodosia Acheson, by now Cadogan, with her husband the diplomat Sir Alexander Cadogan at Westbury, England, in 1916–17 with their dog Benjamin.

A prompt letter of thanks for a Christmas present from the Duke to Alice Stanley, the Duchess's younger daughter and a favorite companion of the Duke's, from on board the SS *Serapis*.

Herbert Hampton

Hampton's statue of the Duke of Devonshire, London

Ferdy's terminology regarding "what Hampton did to your bust" is slightly unfortunate, particularly as there was a family rumor that the sculptor Herbert Hampton (1862–1929) may have had more than a professional interest in May. The Hamptons appear more than once in Ferdy's letters, and were neighbors of the Platts in Maida Vale. The obituary of Herbert Hampton in the *Times* acknowledged his success as the creator of public memorials, including six of Queen Victoria, one of Edward VII in Euston Road, and one of George V in India. Hampton was also the sculptor who created the bronze statue of Spencer Cavendish, 8th Duke of Devonshire, which is sited at the entrance to Horse Guards Avenue, Whitehall, London—thus providing a posthumous link between the duke and his personal physician.

Natives sitting outside a sort of caffee playing some game like draughts. The Nile is quite smooth, not a ripple and the smoke from sugar factory chimneys (horrible blots on the landscape) goes straight up. As I write it is getting darker, the blush on the hills is going, the dynamo is vibrating the lights are turned up and a cool air is coming on board which is grateful after the heat of day which has been higher than usual especially after lunch. The temp was 76° in my cabin. I am writing this sitting on the stern of the boat and using a box of the Duchesses "bathbags" as a writing table. I am close to the dining saloon, the windows of which are open and the native waiters are laying the dinner table and chatting Arabic. I also hear talking on shore and the barking of dogs on the opposite bank, and the occasional weird song in a minor key of the Nile boatmen. We have had beautiful moon light for the last few nights and tonight it is full and will soon rise. I wish you were here to see and enjoy all this and talk about it with me. I find it dull at times. After meals every[one] except Lord G. settles down to books. A train is just passing near the bridge and making a tremendous clatter in the still air.

The D. and Dss. and Lady T. went on shore for a walk. I generally go with Sir C. but he is not going this evening. It is odd how apathetic they all seem to be. I am looking forward to Luxor where we shall probably stay some days, as I shall be able to see more.

I hope you are all well and things going on smoothly. I forgot to say that I was glad you like my portrait. I am curious to know what Hampton did to your bust. Please remember me to them. Give my love to all at No. 10. I hope Lily is better. When is she going to stay with you. My letters and yours have a good way to go to and from Cairo. We sometimes get these sent down river to us by the post boat or express boat, sometimes sent up by those which overtake us. I am going to post this now. It is quite dark.

Much love dearest
Your affectionate husband
Ferdy
(A.F.R. Platt)

For Violet
xxxxx
xxxxx

For Rowly
xxxxx
xxxxx

SS *Serapis* Luxor
Saturday Nov. 30th 1907 9.55 pm

My darling,

Although I posted a letter to you this afternoon I am beginning another now because I want to write down some stories which I heard at dinner tonight told by Sir C.

They were about Lord Marcus Beresford.[1] There were some races somewhere and at 4 am that morning there was a prize fight to which Ld. M.B. [Lord Marcus Beresford] went. The police suddenly appeared and everyone ran away. He had on a red smoking jacket and the chief constable of Hants [Hampshire] pursued him on horseback and caught him. On being asked what he was doing then he said "It was a lovely morning and I was looking out of my window at 4 o'clock when I saw a crowd and went out to see what it was when suddenly the crowd began to run and I ran too"! So they let him go. Coming back from some races once there were <u>seven</u> others in the carriage including a man known as "half crown Jack" who was always losing money and having the brokers in etc. Near the end of the journey we suddenly discovered that he had lost his ticket and wanted to know what he was to do. Thinking someone would lend him the fare. Ld. M.B. however said "well there is only one thing to do and that is to get under the seat and we will throw rugs and coats under it". He then asked every one to give him their tickets. When the collector came round Ld. B. handed them to him. The man said "hello there are eight tickets" "yes" said Lord B. "But there is another gentleman under the seat. He prefers travelling that way". The fact was when he got under and they moved the coats, etc. Ld. B found his ticket and said nothing about it. Some one told Lady G. that his wife was having the drawing room furnished in the style of "one of those fashionable Louis"!

Lady G. was staying somewhere and a lady who was leaving had made out a list of all the tips she was going to give. After distributing them she came in and sat down in the drawing room and said "thank goodness that's over". Then there was a knock at the door and the butler came in and handing her something said "I think ma'am you have made a mistake". It was the list! And now dear that is the end of <u>my</u> list for tonight.

---

1   Lord Marcus Talbot de la Poer Beresford, son of the 4th Marquess of Waterford, was an equerry and manager of His Majesty's thoroughbred stud for both Edward VII and George V. The Beresfords are a family long associated with racing and polo.

Serapis, Luxor
Monday Dec. 2nd 1907 8.30 am

We leave Luxor this morning as soon as the mail is in from Cairo, that is soon after 10.30 am. So I am just send[ing] a few lines before breakfast and before we leave as we may tie up somewhere there is no Post Office I have just heard that we shall get to Esneh today so there will be plenty of time to post there: Yesterday, Sunday, I went to Karnak[1] again and saw some buildings of various periods which I had not seen before.

It is unfortunate that the films for the camera are all bad as I have been unable to take a single photo of anything I wanted. However I am going to write to Kent and ask him to get me some more. Lady T. has taken a good many. She condescended to show them to me last night and will allow me to make lantern slides from the negatives. I am sending a few postcards to Fy. Newton. Will you forward them. There don't seem to be many good ones here. Temples of course are not good subjects: they don't make "pretty" pictures. I have sent Lily one of the best I could find There are several new hotels here at Luxor since '96. The Police have put a stop to begging to a large extent; one has therefore less annoyance from clamours for bakhshish.[2]

2.15 pm We have just finished lunch and I am writing this in pencil because I am sitting in the stern (in a comfortable seat which I have secured!) where the boat vibrates very much. We left Luxor at 11.30 am much to every ones satisfaction I believe as they had exhausted all the sight seeing and were tired of lying against the bank. So here we are on our way up to Esneh. The afternoons always improve the scenery on the Nile as the shadows bring out the details of the hills. It is delightful to bask in the sun and watch the various things as we pass. There are many more sugar factories than formerly and they spoil the scenery with their ugly great chimneys. Another horrible thing about them is that they are always whistling like a railway engine only oftener and longer at a time

---

1   Vast religious complex on the east bank of the Nile at Luxor, centred around a temple to
     the god Amun-Ra.
2   *Bakshish* is a gift of money, routinely requested from tourists in Egypt.

They used to wake me up at Mena House. They seem to imitate cocks crowing and other noises.

5.35 – We are just nearing Esneh (after a lovely sunset and after glow) so I am going to post this as soon as we get ashore. The pink glow in the hills and (inspite of the sun having set) the green, emerald green of the "bursim"[1] and Indian corn was beautiful. The cook is so pleased about his hand and last night he asked me to choose any sweet I fancied so for lunch today we had pudding à la Royale!![2] Only he used biscuit instead of breadcrumbs so it was not quite so good. However next time. This place (Esneh) is swarming with people on both sides of the Nile as they are building a barrage here. The one at Assyut is very large so is this and they seem to quarry a great deal more in the hills all the way up the Nile than they used to do.

I must stop and post this.

Much love darling to you and chicks at No. 18 from
Your loving husband
Ferdy
A.F.R. Platt

SS *Serapis*, Esneh
Wednesday Dec. 4th 1907 8.30am

My darling,

I am hoping to post this before we leave this morning. Yesterday everybody except Sir C. and I went to see the temple in the morning. I have seen it before and it really isn't worth seeing again and so as he wanted to walk in the town I went with him. I am writing this in the smoking room

---

1   Berseem or Egyptian clover (*Trifolium alexandrinum*) is a legume crop grown for fodder.
2   A confection of milk, sugar, butter, flour, and crème anglaise.

as no one is up yet so I can have it all to myself. Sir C. and I went for a walk also before breakfast. One gets out of sorts if one gets no exercise. After lunch a launch came to take us across the river to see the works in progress at the new barrage which is built across the Nile at this spot.[1] In the distance here the place looks like an ants nest with tiny black ants running to and fro. Last year they employed 12,000! men this year they have 5,000. That is only for the digging and moving the mud and sand the others are masons etc. The stuff is carried by men and boys in baskets on their heads or shoulders or in two boxes with a moveable bottom slung on camels.

We were taken round by two men a Mr. Lloyd who represents the Egyptian Government and another whose name we did not catch and who represented John Aird[2] who has the contract. They expect to get it done a year sooner than the contract time. This suits not only J. Aird & Co. but also the Government because whenever this is done they get the value of a whole extra years crop.

We went all over the works saw them digging which is all done by piece work the men who dig and those who carry the soil all get so much a cubic yard or metre between them so it keeps them up to the mark. It is a big place with a number of Europeans the English of course being English have rigged up goal posts for football and a netting pitch for cricket while the staff have a tennis court. At Xmas they have sports for the natives who are very keen to win a few piastres in an obstacle race or for climbing a greasy pole! The men or the D. and ladies were taken around on trolleys and we came back sitting on chairs in a truck with a snorting little engine the John Aird in front. The government man Lloyd has a nice house very high rooms and cool a big garden which is full of shrubs fruit and flowers. It is kept going by the water pumped up from the Nile by the engines in the works. He has pomegranate trees roses etc. also a stork which being

---

1   The Esna Barrage, whose construction was nearing completion in 1907, was one of the last old-style stone barrages across the Nile, designed to regulate the river's flow and expand irrigation.

2   Sir John Aird, Bt (1833–1911), British civil engineer. In 1861, Aird joined the family firm founded by his father (also John) in 1848, and became one of the leading civil engineers of the late nineteenth and early twentieth centuries. Projects undertaken by John Aird & Co. included railways, docks (at Avonmouth, London, and Singapore) and water works, notably the first Aswan Dam (completed in 1902) and the Asyut Barrage (completed a year later).

injured in some way could not fly and has taken up its abode there, he lives on the small frogs of which there are plenty. We all had tea in his house which was very cool. I won't stop to write more as I may miss the post expect to hear from you today.

Much love from your affect. husband
Ferdy
A.F.R. Platt
Xxxxxxxxxxx   Violet
Xxxxxxxxxxx   Boy

SS *Serapis* between Gebel Silsilis and Kom Ombo
11.30 am Friday Dec. 6th 1907

My darling,

I am afraid you will only get one letter this week because I could not post after leaving Esneh as there was no P.O. at Silsilis[1] and I did not know till too late that there was one at Edfu. However you will get one I hope. As we go higher and higher up the Nile letters take longer to go down to Cairo. I expect we shall be at Kom Ombo about 1 o'clock today and at Aswan tomorrow afternoon Saturday 7th. We left Cairo on Thursday Nov 7 so we have been one month on board yesterday.

We arrived at Edfu on Wednesday afternoon and I had just time to go up to the top of the Great Pylon[2] and see the sun set you get a magnificent view of the Nile Valley from the top. Next morning Lord G. called me at 5.45 and we went up together to the top of the Pylon to see the sun rise: 242 steps! After breakfast we all started off at 9 o'clock to see the temple itself. They have done some repairs to it and excavated a small temple in front of it. The D. likes to ask me questions about the temples and hieroglyphics and stars. I examined him this morning he is improving but still short of

---

1   Gebel al-Silsila, a site of sandstone quarries and pharaonic monuments on both sides of the Nile.
2   The main gateway of the Ptolemaic temple.

breath on exertion. We left Edfu in the morning after we returned from the
temple and reached Gebel Silsilis about 4 o'clock. I was delighted to stop
there as on the *Rameses* I've passed it by at 6 or 7 am. It is the narrowest
part of the Nile which is shut in by two hills of sandstone. It is a picturesque
spot. The Anc. Eg. [Ancient Egyptians] quarried most of their sandstone
there and on both sides of the river the rock has been cut away like slices of
cheese or butter leaving great smooth surfaces. There are a great number
of shrines to gods and tombs. We landed and saw some of these. I went
on with the guardian to see some more. I found the tomb of a man named
Amenemhat whose wife's name was [hieroglyphs for *mymy*] which reads
"Mimi", quite a modern sounding sort of pet name. I can now (12 o'clock)
see <u>Kom Ombo</u> from my cabin door as I write. So we shall be there in
about half an hour or less. I expect we shall see the temple after lunch. We
left Silsilis at 9.45 am this morning. We steam about 7 miles an hour which
sounds rather slow. But there would be little charm in tearing along like
a Vanguard.[1] It is very delightful to be out of the noise of London. If this
had been a sailing Dahabeeah[2] with a tug it would have been better still as
there would be no noise at all. The stars are lovely at night now especially
as there is no moon. The Duke is very keen about recognizing them and
always wants to know what they are. He has Sir Robert Ball's[3] story of the
heavens and another work by him (Ball), also Philips Planisphere. Arabella
Buckley's[4] "Short History of Natural Science". So you see he <u>is</u> studying
"<u>science generally</u>"! We are passing the huge chimney stack of the pump-
ing engine which raises the water to irrigate the desert land here which is
being reclaimed by an English Company got up by Sir Ernest Cassel. We
are now stopping opposite it and after lunch we are going to see some of
the work going on. There is a huge engine to be seen, etc.

---

1   A fast boat—now a make of powerboat.
2   More commonly spelled *dahabiya* today, A flat-bottomed, two-masted houseboat, which
     was the craft of choice for well-heeled travelers to Egypt during the nineteenth and early
     twentieth centuries.
3   Sir Robert Stawell Ball (1840–1913), Irish astronomer and professor of astronomy at
     the University of Cambridge, where the Duke of Devonshire was chancellor. Cambridge
     University Press published Ball's book, *The Story of the Heavens*, in 1900.
4   Arabella Buckley (1840–1929), prolific writer and science educator. She was a friend
     of Charles Darwin and her *Short History of Natural Science* was published in 1876.
     The Duke of Devonshire's level of scientific knowledge may have been indicated by the
     book's full title, *A Short History of Natural Science and of the Progress of Discovery
     From the Time of the Greeks to the Present Day.*

Sir Ernest Cassel

Ernest Joseph Cassel (1852–1921) was a British banker of German origin. Born in Cologne, Cassel moved to England at the age of seventeen and went on to make a great fortune as a banker and financier. He specialized in large mining, industrial, and infrastructure projects, including the building of the first Aswan Dam. Cassel became one of the wealthiest men of his time, and counted King Edward VII, Prime Minister Herbert Asquith, and Winston Churchill among his friends. He was much decorated for his services to the British empire. In 1898, Cassel cofounded the National Bank of Egypt. He retired from active financial deals in 1910. His funerary monument, at Kensal Green Cemetery in London, is decorated with a winged sun disc, reflecting his long association with Egypt.

I hope to get a letter if not two today. It will probably come by the post boat down from Assuan. I am longing to hear how you and the children are. 2.45 It is very hot being anchored off the bank at Kom Ombo, this side north of the temple, and the temp. in my cabin is 77°F but being dry one does not feel it so much. I believe some are going to the temple at Kom Ombo in Ld. G.'s boat and others land here to see the works. I don't know which yet. I want you [to] ask your mother if she would mind sending me the next years Walker's Diary now as I should like to keep up my diary. The number stamped inside the cover is 73.

10 pm – The Gosfords went to the temple. I went with the Duke, Duchess and Sir Charles to see the irrigation works. We first went to see the engines and pumps which are enormous each engine pumps up 3 tons a second and there are six at work. We then went on a small railway in little carriages drawn by mules, to see the canal which was filled by the pumps and also the cultivated ground. The cultivated area will be enormous. I forget how many square miles. It will be a good thing for the company, for the government and

the Fellahin who rent the land. We were taken round by Birch Pasha[1] who is at the head of the works, also Sir – Wilcox [Willcocks] who is the engineer who had something to do with the Assuan Dam I believe. He wants to irrigate Mesopotamia only the Sultan is not friendly with England just now so it is difficult to get permission. He is a clever man and good company. He was out in Uganda a short time ago and had had blood poisoning and his face had to be cut in several places and as a result he had facial paralysis on one side. It is getting better but his mouth is still drawn to one side. On our return we went to Birch Pasha's house to tea. Mrs. B[irch] in the morning sent the Duchess a quantity of chrysanthemums and the largest jasmine flowers I ever saw they were as big as stephanotis only not so thick and fleshy of course. The cook's gratitude continues as we had pudding à la Royale again tonight but as he made a sauce flavoured with roses it was rather sickly. I keep my letters open so long in the hope of having something more to add or getting one from you that I don't post as often as I ought. However I shall post this tomorrow any how. I expect we shall get the post tomorrow before we leave for Assuan. Anyhow we shall get it there. It is only 26 miles from here. I believe we are going up to Wadi Halfa. No more tonight.

8.15 am Saturday Dec. 7th – I am writing a few lines before breakfast I am sitting facing the sun and temple of Kom Ombo. Hitherto when we got up in the morning we generally had the sun on our left (facing looking up stream) that is to say as the river runs generally speaking north and south, the sun is in the east on our left but in the place we have moored at the boat's direction is S.E. so for the first time sun has been off my cabin door which opens on the port or left side. As they left the canvas awning down on the sunny side I found it quite cool dressing. So I am sitting in the sun to get warm. Just opposite a large gap in the awning over the paddle box. I find I shall not be able to post this later until I get to Assuan, so when yours come (if in time) I shall add a few lines.

---

1   John Somerville Birch (1861–1913), Welsh civil servant. The Turkish title "pasha" was a high rank in the Ottoman imperial system, typically conferred on senior officials. Birch served the British administration in Egypt in a variety of capacities, and was regarded as one of the ablest of his generation. In 1894 he was in the Egyptian police, and was decorated by the Khedive for his services. By the time of Ferdy's visit to Egypt, Birch was evidently in charge of the irrigation works at Kom Ombo. He later served as British commissioner of the Egyptian state domains, and was further decorated. He died in London in January 1913 and was buried in Denbighshire, north Wales.

Sir William Willcocks

When the Duke of Devonshire's party arrived at Aswan at the end of 1907, construction of the dam across the Nile was in full swing, ready for its opening the following year. The man responsible for this great feat of engineering was William Willcocks (1852–1932), the leading hydrologist–engineer of the Edwardian era. Willcocks had begun his career in India, but it was in Egypt that he made his mark, conceiving the Aswan Dam and supervising the massive extension of irrigated land downstream that the dam made possible. But Willcocks's pride was to be his undoing. Dismayed at the changes to the dam's design instigated by his successors on the project, Willcocks launched a scathing attack on their professional reputation, which resulted in him being convicted for libel in a Cairo courthouse. His distinguished career ended in ignominy and public disgrace.

2.30 pm – I had a quiet morning every one else went out to see some more of Cassel's irrigation scheme. I stopped at home and tried to sketch Kom Ombo. I did not get very much done before the awning came down. They are always having them down and we are absolutely shut in when they are down and can't see anything. They can't keep them down when we are steaming I am thankful to say. I don't know when we start and whether the Duke means to go to the temple before we go. I shall not feel very sorry if we don't. I have seen it before and it is Ptolemaic and Roman therefore not very interesting. I feel that this has been a stupid sort of letter and I am going to stop now and add something after the mail comes in. Much love to you darling and the children. I hope they are both good and that Violet is getting on with her reading and writing.

Your loving husband
Ferdy
A.F.R. Platt

9.45 pm – My dearest I have been devouring your two long chatty letters. They make me feel at home again. I really begin to wish I were. Of course I am looking forward to Abu Simbel[1] and the other things between Assuan and Wadi Halfa which I have not seen but half the pleasure of the trip is spoilt by the want of "kindred spirits" and . . . "well bred indifference" . . . Conversation at meals is rather a trial except when it gives the Duke a chance of telling some interesting story of some well known person. So you see I am not in the least dazzled by my surroundings and really do wish myself home again. I get very little exercise too except by fits and starts. It is too hot in the middle of the day to do much. Today has been cooler. Last night there was probably a thunderstorm somewhere miles away in the south as there were more frequent faint yellowish flashes lighting up clouds low down on the horizon. Soon after sunset tonight there was a beautiful sight. First the river . . . with the . . . palms standing out sharp and bronze green against a peach coloured horizon fading into deep blue above, then Venus looking like a brilliant silver stud and above that to the left the thin white crescent of the moon with the rest of the disc a much fainter shade lit up by the earth's reflection from the sun. Please thank your mother for her letter which came this morning with yours and the weekly *Times*.

There is so much in your letters that it is difficult to know what to select for comment and I expect you prefer <u>my</u> news to remarks about <u>yours</u>. I am very glad to hear Lily is better and that she is going to stay with you. My love to her. I hope she has received the P.C. [postcard] I sent her the other day. If you are pleased with the stove I am sure I shall be; only be sure you make sure the joints are tight. . . .

I am afraid dear little Violet will be disappointed at not getting a birthday letter from me but I did not realize how close it was to the day – so tell her her daddy has not forgotten her. I hope to get her something at Assuan in time for Xmas. I do so want to see you and the chicks. I don't think I could <u>ever</u> come away for so long again as this! I have not seen as much as I wished to. I was afraid that would be the case before I left. However I have seen a good deal.

---

1   The rock-cut temples of Ramesses II at Abu Simbel, one of the great sights of Egyptian Nubia.

I wonder whether you will remember our wedding day. I shall think of you that night. I am writing this in my cabin which is vibrating with the dynamo. It is dull for me after dinner as Lord G. settles down to a book after a little while, ditto Lady T. While the others play bridge. So I sit in my cabin. I very rarely talk to Lady T., she is supercilious and chilling. The letters here brought down from Assuan by the post boat but I can't post till we get there tomorrow. I wonder if Violet knows what a lizard is like. One sees several here. There were some at Mena House almost white, they used to sit still on the white limestone blocks of which the wall of the house is built and at night when the electric light brought out the flies it was only when they suddenly darted after a fly that you could distinguish them from the stone. We have had no mosquitoes for a long time now but the flies are troublesome at times, especially at meals. You would be surprised to see me getting up so early! I am always out of bed by 7 o'clock and sometimes earlier. The morning is the best time of the day. We have had a high wind today which has cooled us down. The temp in my cabin as I write is 63°F. The day before yesterday at 2 o'clock it was 78°F.

I am glad to know you are keeping up your music, at least I presume you are as you played the other night. Your letters generally come pretty regularly once a week now. Being more than 24 hours from Cairo of course your letters take a week or more to get here. I hope Violet enjoyed her birthday. I expect she had fun with the other children. She is very funny and thinks of such odd things: the milk in the teapot and the water butt were curious ideas to get into her head. You don't say anything about her nettle rash in the letters which came today but I hope it is better, and that Boy's eczema is improving. Your two letters were begun on Sunday 24th and Thursday 28th and received today.

8.15 am Sunday Dec. 8th 1907 – Still at Kom Ombo but we leave at 10 o'clock for Assuan. I am writing this at the smoking room table: a luxury I rarely indulge in except before breakfast. The wife of Birch Pasha has just sent a lot of chrysanthemums on board, yellow and mauve: they fill a small foot bath. I am glad your new maid is satisfactory and hope she will continue to be so. I am afraid you won't [get] this letter for a long time as the mail leaves on Monday I think and it can't get to Port Said in time.

I shall send my Xmas letter off in good time at Assuan because I don't know yet where we can post in Nubia. I keep on threatening to close this letter but never do however I am going to do so at once and avoid temptation.

Much love darling
From your affectionate husband
A.F.R. Platt

SS Serapis, Assuan
11 am Tuesday Dec. 10th 1907

My dearest,

This is a very pretty place and greatly improved since I was here in 1896. Photographs don't do it justice as no photo takes in enough to show what is it like. The river here is broken up by granite rocks varying in size from small boulders to big islands, such as Elephantine itself, where we are moored just opposite the town. Consequently we get a very good view of Assuan. If you look in my old Murray or Baedeker's Upper Egypt[1] you will see a map (and possibly a plan) showing how the river is broken up. The town itself is much improved. They have made a long road along the front which for a short distance is planted with trees and flower beds and there is a band stand (in a little garden) which is covered with Bougainvillea. There are several new hotels. First: the Cataract Hotel which over looks the river.[2] If you look at the photo in the smoking room of Assuan you will see a ruined castle (Saracen) sticking up against the skyline. The Cataract

---

1   (John) Murray and (Karl) Baedeker were the two famous and competing publishers of travel guides in Victorian and Edwardian times, between them effectively inventing the genre. Murray's *Handbooks for Travellers* were first published in 1836; the *Handbook for Travellers in Egypt* (by Gardner Wilkinson) appeared in 1847. The series continued after 1915 under new ownership as the Blue Guides. Karl Baedeker's publishing house was founded in Koblenz in 1827, subsequently moving to Leipzig. Its guide to Egypt was published in two parts, *Upper Egypt* and *Lower Egypt*, in 1885.

2   Opened in 1900 as a health resort, the Cataract Hotel swiftly established itself as the premier hotel of Aswan. Agatha Christie stayed there and used it as the point of assembly for her fictional travelers in *Death on the Nile*.

Hotel is just behind that on lower ground. We arrived on Sunday afternoon and after walking all the way down the front we came to the quarters of a native regiment and they were watering the camels. Boy would like to see them. The men wear white turbans with green aigrette sticking up and a green cummerbund – white garments and a khaki jersey. After going back, I left Sir Charles H. with whom I came ashore and walked on to the Cataract Hotel. If you look at the same photo (there is another view in my big album, one in the little album) you will notice that to the left of the Castle and below it there are some rocks which continue down to the river. They are levelling the ground to the left above and utilising the rocks to form a natural rockery and planting grass flowers and shrubs. Some of the rock[s] have hieroglyphic inscriptions and pictures of the writers (or I should say engraved as they are hammered or cut into the granite) so the whole makes a most attractive spot. I had tea on the verandah of the Cataract Hotel and watched the sun set which was magnificent. The small islands and big blocks of granite, rounded and black, standing out sharply against the light, [the] river winding between them and in which were reflected the gradually changing hues of the sky, Venus and the moon becoming brighter and brighter, as the sky above grew a deeper blue. The distant skyline of the western desert hills with great slopes of sand, golden by day but now quite dark in the shadow, all combined to form a most picturesque scene, which I know you would love to see.

Yesterday morning (Monday 9th) I went in to the bazaars with Lady G. and T. and Sir C. We rowed across in the steamer's boat. In the afternoon Lord and Lady G. and I rowed up stream past the rock on Elephantine with the hieroglyphics on it (which you will see in my little album) and above which is the remains of a temple. You can see them in the big photos. We landed round the corner and looked for more inscriptions. Then we rowed across to the other side and walked up to the Cataract Hotel Verandah and met the Duke and Duchess and Lady T. We all had tea there and saw the sun set and Lady G. took a photo for me of the rocks which look like Elephants and which I believe gave the name to the island. We all went down and went back in our boat. They left much too soon to enjoy the full beauty of the scene as the glow on the water had not appeared. At night the view from our boat is pretty as the whole front of Assuan is lit up by oil lamps on the left (north) and electric light in the station on the right. Last night too the tourist steamer *Rameses the Great* was opposite us and her lights added to the general illumination. This morning I went on shore here (Elephantine) and walked up to see the Nilometer[1] and some inscriptions and met some Germans who are excavating and who politely asked me to go round; one speaks good English. The God of the Cataract district is Khnumu – Khnoubis of the Greeks – and his sacred animal was a ram. They have found the shrine or holy of holies in the temple and last week the French who were here discovered the burial place of the sacred rams who were buried in granite and limestone sarcophagi just as were the sacred Bulls of Apis at Saccareh.[2] This is the first time sacred rams have ever been discovered. They were quite late – Ptolemaic – but the faces of the mummied animal was covered with a gold mask and on their heads were wooden crowns also gilded. I think we are going to stay here some time. Everyone likes being here. It is the most picturesque place on the Nile except Philae. We shall go there also to the barrages or Dam.

We have the most delicious little green figs here, so soft and juicy you can eat them skin and all! They were piled up on the desk just as you see them in the wall paintings in the tombs.

[Ferdy includes here a small sketch of piled-up figs.]

I don't know what we do this afternoon but I am going to close this letter and post it today in case of accidents next week but before doing so I am going to wish you a very Merry Xmas and Happy New Year with the children and all at No. 10 where I suppose you will be.

I shall think of you tonight darling.

Your affectionate husband
Ferdy (A.F.R. Platt)

---

1   Device for measuring the height of the Nile, especially the maximum level reached during the annual inundation. The Nilometer on Elephantine comprised a series of rock steps leading down to the water's edge; the walls of the staircase are scored with horizontal lines at regular intervals.
2   Ferdy is referring to the Serapeum, the underground burial vaults of the sacred Apis bulls at Saqqara, discovered and excavated by Mariette at the beginning of the 1850s.

SS *Serapis*, Assuan
Thursday Dec. 12th 1907

My dearest May,

We have been here four and a half days but it seems like a fortnight, although every day seems to have gone so quickly I get quite mixed up about time and days. I forgot to put down the day I wrote to you; consequently I am not sure what I told you in my last [letter]. Sunday Dec. 8th arrived Assuan. Moored off Elephantine Island. Monday bazaars in morning, went out with Gosfords after 4 pm in boat; tea at Cataract Hotel. Magnificent sunset. Tuesday 10th: I don't think I wrote anything about my doings that day. I walked up from the boat to where the Germans are excavating. Civil man took me round; they have discovered the shrine of the God Khnum (in Greek "Knoubis"). He was ram-headed and was the God of the Cataract district. Last March French explorers found the sarcophagi of the Sacred Rams; each ram's head was covered with gold foil. They were of the Ptolemaic Period. The shrine is a little earlier: Nectanebo,[1] the last king but two of the XXXth Dyn. I saw the sarcophagi; the rams of course have been put in the museum at Cairo. In the evening I went for a walk and had tea at the Cataract Hotel and saw the beautiful sunset again. I have not bought anything for Violet so far, as everything is so expensive. I am sorry to say that she would not get it till after Xmas . . . owing to parcels going by long sea. So I think I had better bring anything back with me. Yesterday we all went off in a Government Steam launch up the river through the beautiful Cataract scenery to the Nile Dam. We went through three locks on the west side. Enormous things. We then were taken right across the dam itself on trolleys to the other (east) side of the river (you see we do a good deal of "trollying"!).

We lunched with the engineer and his wife. Both Scotch and plenty of it! He is a sharp-witted man, quite young. After lunch we went in the launch

---

1   Nectanebo I, first king of the Thirtieth Dynasty (reigned 380–362 BC).

to the temple of Philae.[1] Poor thing! It is very forlorn, two fore courts quite submerged. On the opposite island Reisner was at work but I had no chance of going there. However one of the engineers has asked me to breakfast tomorrow morning and will take me over to see Reisner. I have heard through Alan Gardiner,[2] a young Egyptologist who I met on Elephantine two days ago (and who kindly gave my card to Miss Abel the next day), that Dr. R[eisner] would be glad to see me, also Miss Abel. I ride over about 7 am and get there about 8 in the cool part of the day and we go across in the launch.

This morning I got up at 6.30, shaved, bathed and breakfasted . . . left the *Serapis* in our rowing boat at 7.30 and went down to the Grenfell tombs,[3] which are so called because Gen. Grenfell opened them (Budge actually did it. Badly!). I left about eleven so had a good morning's work! I met young Gardiner again and had a talk with him. To my great joy a letter from you has just been handed to me (7.15) which I must read before dressing for dinner so I must stop.

. . .

Friday Dec. 13th 1907 9.15 pm – I forgot to tell you what a wonderful sight it was to see the Nile rushing through one half [of] the sluices, great clouds

---

1   Temple complex, located on an island at the First Nile Cataract, just south of Aswan. Philae was generally regarded as the most picturesque spot on the Nile (see Ferdy's letter of December 10th). Lovers of Egypt therefore bewailed its fate when the construction of the first Aswan Dam led to parts of the temple being flooded. Following the building of the Aswan High Dam, the whole island was submerged and the temple buildings were relocated to a neighboring island.

2   Alan Gardiner (1879–1963), British Egyptologist. A young man at the time of Ferdy's meeting, Alan Gardiner went on to become perhaps the most eminent British Egyptologist of the twentieth century. His *Egypt of the Pharaohs* remained the defining history of ancient Egyptian civilization for half a century, while his *Egyptian Grammar*, published in the 1940s, is still the standard work on the ancient Egyptian language. But Gardiner was never far from controversy. He famously described ancient Egyptian religion as "loads of mythological rubbish" and, despite his society connections and considerable private means (his translations of ancient Egyptian texts are littered with the upper class terminology of "banquets" and "butlers"), he was placed under house arrest during the Second World War as a Nazi sympathizer.

3   The Grenfell tombs were so called because they were opened by Field Marshal Lord Grenfell (1841–1925), when sirdar (commander of the army in Egypt). Ferdy's barb about Budge's contribution is also hinted at in Arthur Weigall's *A Guide to the Antiquities of Upper Egypt*, which refers to "The tombs of the Prince of Elephantine, sometimes called the Grenfell tombs owing to the fact that some of them were opened by Sir Francis Grenfell (assisted by Dr Budge) in 1885."

of spray rising and the water boiling and tearing along. The reason they are using only one half of the sluices is that they are going to raise the height of the dam, and they are beginning on one side first to stop the water; while they go down to the foundations they let down the gates, mark a square enclosure in front of the dam of sand higher than the water and then pump the water out inside. This morning I went over to the dam, breakfasted with Mr. McCorquodale the resident engineer, went round with him to some of the works and in about an hour's time started off in the steam launch to Dr. Reisner's Dahabeeyeh, where I saw Miss Abel.

After a short talk with her and a young man named Scott, who belongs to the survey depart[ment], and who is surveying Reisner's work for the Gov-[ernment], we went over to the island of Hesseh [Heisa], where Reisner was. McCorquodale and I were lucky, as they had just found a lot of mummies in rock tombs cut out in disintegrated granite. They were of the Ptolemaic Period and apparently priests and priestesses of Isis from the temple of Philae. The faces were gilt and the decorations and paintings were in perfect condition though not very good in style. Dr. Elliot Smith,[1] Professor of Anatomy at Cairo, was examining a number of skeletons from another and later burial ground (about AD 400). There was one case of gout! The man was not Egyptian. Probably he was a bibulous old Roman who did himself too well!

I went into several of the other tombs I mentioned first, and it was strange to see the sandstone sarcophagi with the shrivelled remains of garlands on the top. Owing to the dam the burials in the lower levels of the island have in the course of the last five years been quite spoilt by the damp and infiltration of water. And that is what has happened about the dam for a hundred miles. Every perishable thing in a tomb has been or eventually will be destroyed, if that tomb happens to be in a spot which is now below or near the present high water mark – Dam!

After this we took Reisner and Elliot Smith and the doctor back to his Dahabeeyah and I just said good bye to Miss Abel and went back to the dam, had lunch with McCorquodale and then jogged along back to Assuan on my donkey, visiting the granite quarries on the way – with the old obelisk which was never quite cut out. I get rather tired after these long days

---

1   Grafton Elliot Smith (1871–1937), Australian anatomist and anthropologist. One of the leading authorities on the brain, he worked extensively in Egypt, becoming an expert on mummification. Perhaps his best known work was an investigation of the ancient Egyptian royal mummies.

and sleep like a top and wake early but I don't feel fit for much letter writing till after dinner, and as we dine late I soon get sleepy and ready for bed about 10.30. There is so much to do in the day that I don't get much time to write to any one except yourself and that is not always easy. Miss Abel looks a poor delicate sort of thing but she says she is pretty well; I think she makes the best of herself. She is probably in the best possible place for her lungs. Reisner was civil but he is rather abrupt and not highly polished. I must stop for this is going over to the post. A Merry Christmas darling to you and the chicks; give my love to all at No. 10 and tell them I <u>can't</u> write, I simply don't get the time as long as this sight seeing continues, but I hope to send a line next week.

Much love from your affectionate husband
Ferdy
(A.F.R. Platt)

George Reisner

George Reisner (standing second from left) during excavations at Giza in 1938

Squat, bespectacled, and pipe-smoking, George Andrew Reisner (1867–1942) stands head and shoulders above the rest in the annals of twentieth-century American Egyptology. When Ferdy met Reisner, he was Assistant Professor of Egyptology at Harvard, and preparing to undertake an archaeological survey of Nubia for the Egyptian government. But it was at Giza that Reisner was to make his greatest discovery, uncovering the tomb of Queen Hetepheres, mother of the builder of the Great Pyramid, with her magnificent jewelry and gilded furniture. Reisner's other singular achievement was as head football coach of Purdue University, where in his one season he set a new record. For the last thirty-two years of his life he was Curator of Egyptian Antiquities at Boston's Museum of Fine Arts, transforming its collection into one of the finest in the world.

Ernest Budge

Ernest Alfred Thompson Wallis Budge (1857–1934) was interested in Egyptian and oriental history from a young age, having joined the British Museum in 1883 and subsequently being appointed the first keeper of Egyptian and Assyrian antiquities. He traveled many times to Egypt and Mesopotamia, acquiring many thousands of objects for the museum. He was a prolific author, publishing over 140 separate books and editions, some of which—notably *The Mummy,* 1894—helped to popularize Egyptology. In memory of his wife, Budge established two Egyptological funds at the universities of Cambridge and Oxford, which have supported research and teaching in the discipline for over eighty years.

SS *Serapis* Assuan Island of Elephantine
6.30 pm Wednesday Dec. 18th 1907

My dearest,

I was very happy to get your letter last night which you wrote on <u>the</u> 10th; yes it <u>was</u> very hot at Bath! I found it very hot here too on the 10th, only it was <u>dry</u> heat, quite a <u>different</u> thing! I thought of you dear.

    I often wish myself back at home. I am interested in what I see but I long to be home. I get tired of this cramped existence on board. I cannot get over to the Assuan side at any time as the boat is not always available for me and it costs money to hire one; not much but still money goes very fast in boats and donkeys. People who come out here are all well off and spoil the place for a poor man by scattering their money about too freely. Elephantine is not pleasant to walk alone on as part of it is cultivated, part of it is being excavated and is dusty, and at the other end is the Savoy Hotel. I have been to the Savoy twice to call on Sir Stephen MacKenzie, the brother of Sir Morel

[Morell] MacKenzie. I don't think I mentioned it before. I met him on board the Caledonian being introduced by Dr. Wakeling, the Dr. at Mena House . . . Had tea and a cigar. He has lived out here several winters owing to his asthma. I don't know whether I have told you all this before but I forget what I write and what I have done. The days pass like dreams here. He is a pleasant, unassuming man. He knows a great many people and is going to introduce me to Prof. Sayce,[1] who is the President of the Soc. Bib. Arch. [Society of Biblical Archaeology] when he comes out, if I am here at the time. I have written a short paper for the society on the origin of the name of Elephantine, but I shall submit it to Sayce if possible before I send it in.

The Savoy Hotel is situated in a huge garden with plenty of trees, shrubs and flowers, with plenty of paths, while the Cataract Hotel, although it has river views, is built on the granite rocks and has no garden worth mentioning. Sir S.M. [Stephen MacKenzie] has asked me to go and see him often. He told me that the evidence of that man who said Sir Morel [Morell] MacKenzie went down to Welbeck to introduce him to the D[uke] of Portland was untrue, not only because his brother was only 18 at the time but someone in his family would have known about it, and especially as he and his brother are both in the same profession. The Druces must be very much worried over the affair. I can quite understand Druce himself refusing to open the grave; he is a very obstinate man I should think. Of course the D[uke] of P[ortland] was a very odd man, wore wigs and hid himself, etc., all of which was a good foundation for mysterious lies to be built upon. No one here believes a word of it. I hope they will prosecute the rogue who is at the bottom of it all and has induced the wretched servants to put their money into a rotten concern. I have written to Erny and sent cards to various people. I was glad to hear from you that Minnie is going on well. Tell Violet that people here don't say good morning but "Naharak Said".[2] Hope she is getting on with her lessons. How is the nettle rash? I hope Rowley's eczema is better. He seems to eat well. I hope they chew their food. I do wish Lily was better. I dare say being at No. 18[3] will do her good.

---

1   The Reverend Archibald Henry Sayce (1845–1933), British Assyriologist and philologist. After visiting Egypt in the 1880s, Sayce fell in love with the Nile Valley. In 1891, he resigned his chair at the University of Oxford, bought a *dahabiya*, and spent the next eighteen winters on the Nile, copying inscriptions, meeting Egyptologists, and entertaining visitors.

2   "Good day" in Arabic.

3   That is, back at the Platts' family home, 18 Hall Road, in Maida Vale, West London.

Sir C.H. got a professional photographer to do the *Serapis* and make them into post cards. He ordered a number of them and gave some to everybody including the servants. I have two and send you one. The men on the left below are the sailors; the man above on the left is the Dragoman, whose name is Selim. He speaks English very well of course and is a Syrian from Beyrout [Beirut]. I don't enjoy the heat very much in the middle of the day but it gets cooler at night. It was 82° yesterday at 2 o'clock and 72° at night. Today there has been a pleasant breeze which has made it comfortable. I don't get enough exercise. Must dress for dinner now.

The Druce Portland case

A 1907 sketch from L'Illustration of the Portland trial, demonstrating the international interest in the trial

The Druce Portland case was the great and long-lasting tabloid scandal of the times, and references to it pepper Ferdy's letters. It was based on a fantasy that the reclusive and eccentric 5th Duke of Portland, who disliked being seen and who was responsible for a tunnel-building program at his home Welbeck Abbey—and who used elaborate means to obscure his activities and movements both there and at his London residence—had led a double life as Thomas Charles Druce, a London businessman, who had fathered a succession of children in and out of wedlock. Some twenty years after the death of the 5th Duke of Portland, descendants of Druce, with the assistance of various mountebanks and tricksters, sought to prove, with a company formed for that express purpose, that they were the heirs to the Portland fortune. In 1907 the charade ended when the grave of T.C. Druce was opened and his remains were found to be intact, confounding the plaintiffs' claim that his burial had been faked. Ferdy's distant brush with the case was his meeting and friendship with Sir Stephen Mackenzie (1844–1909). Both Sir Stephen and his brother Sir Morell Mackenzie (1837–1892) were leading physicians of their time, and Sir Morell's name had been introduced into the Druce Portland case by one of the fraudsters who claimed that Sir Morell had introduced him to the Duke of Portland. As Ferdy tells May in his letter, this would have been impossible, as Sir Morell was only eighteen years old at the time of the supposed introduction.

Thursday Dec. 19th 9.15 am

Just finished breakfast. I don't want you to think that I am suffering from the heat or that I am getting <u>no</u> exercise. The heat is not so very bad and I do get some exercise. I sent you a photo showing a view from the Cataract Hotel and I also described the sunset. I went up again the night before last to see it. I never get tired of the sight. It is rather amusing that since I began this morning to write about the heat the temperature has fallen a good deal owing to a strong north wind which is blowing the sand across the river. I had a tooth taken out last Saturday. It was a wisdom in the lower jaw which Barrett stopped. He thought it was dead, but some time after we left Cairo it began to ache. The stopping had come out. At Luxor Sir C.H. had a very loose tooth taken out by the native doctor at the Government hospital. I went with him but he was afraid to tackle mine so I had [to] go on till I came here. It did not bother me always.

The man who took it out was a dapper little German who looked more like a Frenchman. He can't speak English so he had his wife in all the time to translate. I did not want to have it broken off at the crown and then bother with the stumps if they were left in. So I asked if I could have gas but that was not possible. So I said I would have nothing and told him to fire away. However he injected cocaine in the gum in case he had trouble with the roots but it came out quite easily. So I know now that I shan't be in misery on the way up to Wadi Halfa and no dentist within a couple of hundred miles. The one excitement here is to see a tourist steamer arrive or a post boat. Besides those of Cook there are others of the "Hamburgh and Anglo-American" Line – three deckers with stern wheels. They don't seem to do as much as Cook's boats. I have an idea always that my letters are not what you expect. I mean that I tell you things which you don't want to know rather than those which you do. I wish you would let me know the things you like to hear about. I don't think I have any more news at present but I won't keep it open till I hear from you again.

I shall be very very glad to see you again darling.

Much love dearest and to the chicks
Your loving husband
Ferdy
A.F.R. Platt

SS *Serapis* Assuan
7.15 am Tuesday Dec. 24th Xmas Eve 1907

My dearest,

I am rich in letters this week, two from you and one from Lily. I am very sorry I disappointed Violet and that I have mixed up my dates in such a stupid way. I was unable to get anything in the Bazaar until it was too late. Everything I saw was too expensive. However I have bought her a doll. I was pleased to see that she had learned to make pot hooks, etc. so well. You need not worry about that haricot bean; Boy will be all right. I am sorry Lily had to leave you so soon. I thought it would have done her much good if she had stayed with you a month. I think you ought have the dining room chimney seen to unless you are quite certain that the smoke is only due to want of cleaning, because it would be a pity to have the new paint blackened again; you must find the stove a great comfort. I wish we could have one in the dining room too: just in front of the window to warm the cold air.

Since I last wrote I have been taking lots of exercise in the desert, which is most picturesque here on the east side. I go right up the rocky valleys and onto the plateaus above. Yesterday afternoon I started off after lunch and did my longest walk so far. I followed the wild granite gorges up and down till I got into the valley where the railway runs to Shellal, that is south of and above all the rocks and rapids of the 1st Cataract.[1] I walked along the railway to the station, getting there a little before sunset. Shellal has a temporary but fairly numerous population as they are busy there working and quarrying the granite rock for stones to raise the height of the dam. Consequently there is a collection of all sorts of boats by the water, sailing, native boats and steam boats. Sheds and tents for the European workmen (masons), mostly Italians, and the English overseers. I had to wait nearly three quarters of an hour for the 6 o'clock train back to Assuan. But the first

---

1   There are six cataracts (stretches of rapids) between Aswan and Khartoum. The First Cataract, just south of Aswan, includes the islands of Elephantine and Sehel, and formed Egypt's southern border throughout pharaonic history.

thing I did was to go into a general store and bar combined kept by an Italian and get a big drink! You can imagine that after a long walk in the desert one gets very thirsty and one's lips and throat get dry. The shop had a few tables and chairs in front, a counter, glass-fronted cases of macaroni in all shapes, beans, etc., shelves behind with Chianti, Vermouth, etc., etc. I had some horrible tea, but a good dose of good whiskey (Black and White) and soda. I then walked about and smoked and watched the sun set, which was very fine. The rounded boulders of granite on the skyline of the islands and hills look at a distance rough and jagged and stood out well against bright sky.

The immediate surroundings consisted of mounds of earth on which I stood, a native bazaar of mud sheds (which will disappear when the works are finished), hobbled donkeys, stray dogs, geese being driven into the water, a native policeman, a string of camels moving slowly along long rows of hewn granite blocks waiting to be loaded on the boats, a broken Sakkiyeh,[1] railway carriages and the station, and the natives going home. The sky became more and more beautiful and things began to look less distinct. Out in the Nile was poor half-drowned Philae looking quite sad and out of place in all these horribly modern surroundings, and by way of a final touch to the contrast, as soon as the sun had set, the rocks began to echo the dull sullen roar of numerous blasting charges of dynamite in all directions. At six pm the train started and I reached the boat about 6.40. The stars were very bright.

3 pm – Since I began this I walked in the same direction this morning and saw several unfinished sarcophagi still lying in the quarries, an inscription of Amenhotep III[2] and a statue of Osiris[3] all cut in the granite. The statue is lying on its back and is unfinished but the face is cut out. The head faces S.E. in the direction of Shellal with its cranes and boats, blasting, railway lines, telegraph poles and other evidences of civilisation. There it lies with its arms folded across the chest, with a quiet patient expression in its eyes which are turned up to the bright blue cloudless sky and the bright sand stone rocks above it looking orange by contrast. A hundred feet below where the granite ends is the flat valley across which stalks the telegraph

---

1   A *saqiya* (as it is more usually spelled) is a waterwheel, usually driven by oxen.
2   Ninth king of the Eighteenth Dynasty (reigned c. 1390–1353 BC), and one of the most prolific builders in ancient Egyptian history.
3   The ancient Egyptian god of the dead, resurrection, and fertility.

poles, beyond that the eternal desert hills. And as I stood up there alone with Osiris in the fierce sun this Xmas Eve I thought of those lines:

From out his vision vast
The early gods have passed,
They waned and perished with the faith that made them[1]

And that he would probably lay there until railway and telegraph poles have "perished with the civilisation that made them".

This is unpleasant paper to write on, it is so slippery, especially when writing on my knee in my cabin. The Xmas tree is being decorated behind the funnel or I should say on the shore side. I don't go near it as no one has mentioned it. I was asked by Lady G. last Sunday evening if I would care to go with her and Lord G. for a sail in his boat the Ibis. I was surprised as I have never been asked before and as I have said, although they are all very civil they keep one at a distance. The sun was setting and it was cool. We sailed up past the Cataract Hotel and it was quite dark when we returned. It was very pleasant and the stars were so bright. At night we don't see the stars at their best because there is so much light on board.

I wrote to Jim some time ago. I hope he had my letter. Everything is very expensive out here, especially washing soap, matches and tobacco and hair cutting, nearly double. Tea at a hotel costs about 1/3d. I had some nails put into a pair of boots which cost 9d. It costs 7½d to cross in a small boat to the other side. The Savoy Hotel however runs a launch and boats for which you pay nothing. I don't know when we go to Wadi Halfa but it must be soon. I have been enquiring at Cook's office here about the P&O boats. I have [the] idea that it would be better to come home by long sea all the way to London and so avoid the sudden change of temperature and the railway journey. Of course it would be longer – 2 weeks; what do you think? The following are a list of the boats and dates of sailing from Port Said.

India	7911	tons	Jan. 20
+*Oceana*	6610	"	" 27
+*Mongolia*	9500		Feb. 3
Egypt	7912		Feb. 10

1   From Henry Newbolt's poem "The Nile."

I expect it will be one of the two I have marked. They all go to Marseilles.

I shall think of you and all at No. 10 tomorrow night at dinner and will drink your health in champagne, but I am afraid it will not be a very "merry" Xmas for me.

Xmas Day

Last evening we had a grand function with the Xmas tree. I was lying down on my bed about 6 pm for a rest, when there was a knock at the door and the Duke's voice, "Will you come and see the Xmas tree?" The presents were all laid out on tables, not hung on the tree, which had a lot of other things. The Duke presented me with an Agate match box, which Lady G. I fancy bought in the Bazaar as I saw several there. It is nickel mounted and the stone is stained blue. It resembles the box Aunt Emily gave me, only it is not moss-agate, just the ordinary banded agate. It is rather large. I expect it came from Germany. Lady G. gave me a Japanese ashtray of metal enamelled. Lord G. heard me say I had no diary for next year or this (we were talking about Whitaker[1] and the rising and setting of stars) so he gave me a couple of Letts diaries 1907 and 1908. This morning the whole boat has been decorated with palm branches outside on the rails and arches over the companion and in the dining room. You can imagine how delighted I was to receive a letter from you last evening, especially as it was Xmas eve. I was very interested to get your cuttings from the M[orning] P[ost] about the Druce case. I don't see why D.[Druce] should open the grave to please rogues but he has done the correct thing in offering to do so if the rogues themselves are prosecuted! I was amused with Lily Brayton's[2] speech. You may be amused with it still more if you will take "As you like it" and look at the epilogue of which her speech is a parody.

I forgot to mention that all the crew appeared one after another and received something from the Duchess's hand (which one man kissed by the way). It was tobacco mostly. It was comic to hear the dragoman as masters

---

1   Whitaker's Almanack, a compendium of astronomical and other information, published annually since 1868.
2   Lily Brayton (1876–1953), English actress and singer known for her performances of Shakespeare, and her nearly two thousand appearances in the Great War hit musical Chu Chin Chow. It is not clear whether the speech to which Ferdy refers is related to the Druce Portland case.

of the ceremonies introduce them. "This is the head waiter," "This is the ironing man" (washer man), "This is a sailor" (which like the others was perfectly obvious). One of two small boys who sail a boat in which the D. etc. have often sailed was "commanded" to appear. He was announced by the name of his boat, "This is the Puritan," which was still more amusing.
. . .

I am longing to get home. I want a warm heart and I find Tennyson's line very appropriate just now, "Kind hearts are more than coronets".[1] Much love darling, and kisses to the chicks.

From your loving husband
Ferdy
A.F.R. Platt

SS *Serapis* Assuan
9 am Friday Dec. 27th 1907

My dearest,

We leave here tomorrow, Saturday, and I am sending you a few lines in case of accidents. I had a letter from you last night begun on the 19th, such a long one. I do so look forward to your handwriting. I also received your mother's note with the diary, and am writing to her today. We are still getting those nice little figs, but I expect they will come to an end now we are leaving Assuan. I have written a letter to Violet which [I] hope will please her. Today they move the boat over to the opposite bank, that is the Assuan side, as they want to coal before we leave. So everyone is going to clear out after breakfast. The Duke asked me to go with them to the dam, where they will sail about in the government launch and have lunch at the dam, but I am going to stop and go for a walk with Sir C.H. and have lunch at one of the hotels. . . . Thank you for the *Times*. I am longing to hear the end of the Druce case.

---

1   From Alfred, Lord Tennyson's poem "Lady Clara Vere de Vere."

I drank your health silently at dinner the other night (Xmas day) in champagne, also all the rest of the family. I did wish I could have been with you. I wish poor Violet could lose that nettle rash altogether. Boy seems to be much better.

I shall not be sorry to go on tomorrow, although I have enjoyed the walks in the desert very much, but I can't do anything else, everything costs so much money. I wanted to go to the west side in a boat and keep it waiting for me but they asked six shillings! I intended to go and see an old ruined Coptic monastery and possibly some of the tombs which I had seen before. As soon as I know what boat I am to leave Egypt in I will write and tell you at once. I have nothing more to tell you at present but I may write tomorrow before we leave. . . .

Much love to you darling from
Your loving husband
Ferdy
(A.F.R. Platt)

SS Serapis – Dakkah, Nubia
New Year's Eve 8.30 am Dec. 31st 1907

My dearest,

Just a few hurried lines as we expect the boat from Wadi Halfa any minute which will take our letters down. I will write a longer letter next time. We left Assuan at 2 pm.

It took a long time to get through the locks as this boat only just fitted in. I think I told your mother in my last letter that everything was changed the other day and instead of a walk with Sir C. we were both suddenly commanded by the Duchess to attend her "Picnic at the Dam". He rode on with the Duke the Duchess and Lady G. in a carriage. The rest followed on donkeys. The D.'s donkey went lame about a mile from the dam and I got off mine and put him on it and walked. I was very glad as I wanted a walk. We had lunch in Cooks "rest house" and then had a sail in the steam launch. We had tea at MacDonald's, the chief engineer, then home on donkeys again. After we passed the locks we went over to Shellal to coal by which time it was sunset. Shellal is the railway terminus opposite Philae and where I was the other day so I enjoyed it immensely. The rocky islands and palms look so well in the sunset.

Next morning Lady G. went off to see Reisner's work some little way up the river; as she didn't ask me to go with her I missed it. The Survey Department sent down a steam dahabiyeh for her. (The express boat seems a long while coming so I will go on having also had my breakfast.) After Lady G. had gone it was arranged that we were to follow up and take her on board. Just as we started Winston Churchill on board a steamer came down the river on his way back from Uganda etc. He came on board with a Col. Gordon Wilson and his secretary Marsh and we then went on up the river to take Lady G. on board; after that we all had lunch.

He showed us a great number of photographs and told us much that was interesting about the places he had been to. I can't stop to tell you all I heard but he said the crocodiles below the Victoria Falls on the Zabesie [Zambezi] were very numerous.

They waited there for fish and other animals which came over the falls and which were killed by the fall. When anything fell into the water the whole bank appeared to fall in too that meant that thousands of crocodiles were jumping in the water. W.C. [Churchill] and the others enjoyed their lunch as they had not had such a good one for a long time! He was impressed with the Gordon College at Kartoum. There was a tribe in Central Africa which wore no clothing and also were most virtuous but directly a woman began to wear clothes she went wrong!

The scenery up here is very wild and picturesque great sandstone, basalt and granite rocks close to the water edge for miles. All the same there are a great number of small villages at intervals, and the people cultivate the wretched strip of soil between the river and desert.

It is sad to see the dead or dying pelicans all the way up beyond the dam. All the people have been compensated but they cling at least a good many of them to their old homes instead of going to Egypt or farther south. In three years' time when the dam is completed the water will be 17 feet higher and then they will have to clear out. Although the dam has thrown a good deal of land out of cultivation, for about 100 miles in Nubia it is thought that tracts of land and basins which were too high to get any water will now be inundated, and will really give employment to a greater number of fellahin than before and bring in a greater revenue.

After lunch (on Sunday) Winston Churchill's steamer came up and took him and the others off and we steamed up the Nile. It is odd that Erny met him in the Khyber Pass 10 years ago and now I have met him at the 1st Cataract. We tied up for the night at Kertassi, where there is a small ruined Ptolemaic temple.[1] As soon as I could get ashore I started off into the desert up the sandstone rocks to catch the last rays of the setting sun but the crest of the hill only gave me a view of another farther off and higher. However I had a good week and enjoy these walks in the desert very much. The air is so dry and bracing.

Yesterday, Monday 30th, we left Kertassi and steamed through a very wild gorge, high granite and basalt rocks shutting in the river. At one spot there was a small bay with a narrow strip of land bright emerald green with a young crop just coming up and palm trees forming an agreeable contrast to the bold rocky cliffs. The castor oil plant is abundant here, also henna, which the people of Egypt and the East use to dye their fingernails an orange-red colour as well as garments. At the end of this gorge we came to Kalabsheh, where there are two temples, one big and late (Ptolemaic and Roman) the other known as the Beit El Walli, small and of the time of Rameses II and therefore much finer than the other in the matter of sculpture. The Beit El Walli is cut out of the hillside. We then went on again and moored at Dakkeh, where there is another late temple of no interest. Lord G. and I walked out into the desert for about ¾ hour till it got dark. Just before dinner Cook's tourist steamer *Prince Abbas* came up and moored alongside. She left for Wadi Halfa early next morning, that is this morning. Soon after breakfast we started and crossed over to a small place where there is a telegraph office. It is the landing place for Stores, etc. of the Nile Valley Co., which is working the gold mines about 100 miles off in the desert in the Wadi Alaki. We saw great cigar-shaped tins for water and the camels which carried it out to the mines for the men there. After the Duchess had sent off some telegrams we left and now (11.15) we are on our way to Wadi Sabua.

---

1   In fact, the small kiosk at Qertassi is early Roman in date, probably contemporary with
       Trajan's kiosk at Philae.

Winston Churchill, Eddie Marsh, and Colonel Gordon Wilson

Winston Churchill (front row, left center) and Eddie Marsh (front row, right center) in Uganda in 1907

Winston Churchill traveled to inspect Britain's holdings in East Africa while serving as undersecretary of state for the colonies. The book which resulted was *My African Journey*, a classic which remains in print. Winston Churchill requires no introduction, but the wider cultural importance of his secretary, Eddie Marsh (1872–1953), will probably only be known to students of English literature. Marsh became Churchill's private secretary in 1905, when Churchill was appointed under-secretary of state for the colonies, beginning an association and friendship that would last until Marsh's death. Marsh was to work with Churchill until 1929, and thereafter was private secretary to every secretary of state for the colonies until Marsh retired in 1937. His literary life was led in parallel. He was the friend of many poets, and edited five anthologies of *Georgian Poetry* between 1912 and 1922. He was Rupert Brooke's literary executor, having earlier introduced the poet to Siegfried Sassoon. Marsh was also a collector of the works of avant-garde artists associated with the Bloomsbury Group, and was a close friend of Ivor Novello. He was a discreet but influential figure in early twentieth-century homosexual circles in Britain.

Churchill's other companion on the *Serapis* was Colonel Gordon Wilson, who had married Churchill's aunt Lady Sarah Spencer-Churchill. Wilson had been aide-decamp to Robert Baden-Powell (founder of what would become the World Scout Movement) at the Seige of Mafeking in the Boer War, and Lady Sarah accompanied him there. While there, she was recruited by Alfred Harmsworth to cover the seige for the *Daily Mail*, thus becoming almost certainly the first woman war correspondent. Her adventures were nearly as hair-raising as those of her nephew Winston, who was Boer War correspondent for the *Morning Post*. Gordon Wilson returned to active service on the outbreak of the Great War and was almost immediately killed, in November 1914, while in command of a charge of the Royal Horse Guards.

I shall stop now and hand this letter to the dragoman ready to catch the boat, but before doing so I must wish you a very happy New Year and also the chicks and all at No. 10.

The Duchess told me yesterday that they would be back at Cairo on the 28th and as soon as I know what boat I am coming by I will let you know.

With much love dearest to you and the children
Always your loving husband
Ferdy
(A.F.R. Platt)

SS *Serapis* between Abu Simbel and Wadi Halfa
Thursday Jan. 2nd 1908 2.45 pm

My dearest,

I have spoken to the Duke and am going to leave Port Said by the *Mongolia* (9,500 tons) on Feb 3rd. I have decided to come by long sea, all the way, as the change will not be so sudden. Lord G. has advised me to do so too. I think it takes about a fortnight from Port Said to London but of course I will let you know later on.

We left Dakkeh on Tuesday 31st 10.15 am and arrived at Korosko at sunset. There are some fine rugged hills a few hundred yards from the Nile and some of us started to climb one but it became too dark to get to the top, which was a pity because there is a fine view to be had from there. We left the next morning at 6 am for Abu Simbel (before I went to bed however Sir C. and I and the D. had drinks and wished each other a Happy New Year. I silently drank yours) and arrived there about 4.30 pm and went inside the great Temple which is lit up by electricity, but the current is supplied from the steamer! It is an easy matter as the temple is so close to the river. Unfortunately the light is not very strong. However I saw what I wanted to. The statues of the king both inside and out are very impressive.

I afterwards climbed to the top of the hill which is very steep and covered with deep golden sand which makes it very hard work. The sun had set sometime when I reached the top but I had a magnificent view, the Nile winding away in the distance upstream and downstream among the desert sandstone hills, many of which are isolated and look like pyramids. The top of the hill or I should rather say chain of hills is almost flat in some places and is covered with pieces of sand-worn and sand-polished black basalt and flat pieces of heavy Indian red sandstone. One could see for miles. It was getting dark and the scene, although picturesque, was a lovely one and I thought with longing for home, for I am rather lonely on board except when I have an occasional chat with Lord Gosford or Sir C. Down below out of sight was the *Serapis* and the tourist boat *Prince Abbas*, but although I could not see them I could hear (from the latter) the strains of a piano which although very jingly seemed somehow a link with home and the kind hearts which are more than coronets.

Next morning (that is this morning Jan. 2nd Thursday) Lord G. and I got up early and saw the sun rise and enter part of the temple. If we had come a few weeks later we should have seen the sun's rays pass right to the end wall of the sanctuary and fall on the Altar and light up the four figures which have been sitting there for more than 3,000 years.[1] The figures represent from left to right Ptah, Amen-Ra, Rameses II and Harmachis (Heru-m-akhti). I saw with interest in the little shrine to the left of the temple the names of McCallum,[2] the artist who discovered it, and Amelia Edwards. I also went inside the smaller temple which was excavated for the favourite wife of Rameses II – Nefertari – in honour of the Goddess Hathor. About 10.45 we left. I was sorry we had so little time as I should have liked to have seen more. We stayed nearly 3 weeks at Assuan, where there is nothing much do after a week of it, but at Abu S[imbel] we were only a few hours!

I am sitting in my usual place at the stern of the boat and you will be glad to hear that I have a cushion. It has not been so very hot in Nubia. My cabin is usually about 72° at this time of day and as we are moving get a breeze and the air is so dry one does not feel the heat. It being New Year's Day we had Plum Pudding again and again I <u>drank</u> to you in champagne. There is champagne going every night but I always drink claret.

---

1   The temples of Abu Simbel were built by Ramesses II, third king of the Nineteenth
     Dynasty (reigned c. 1279–1213 BC).
2   Andrew McCallum (1821–1902), British landscape painter who made several trips to
     Egypt between 1870 and 1875. His paintings are widely represented in national collec-
     tions. Queen Victoria commissioned him to paint landscape views near Balmoral.

Amelia Edwards

A popular Victorian novelist, Amelia Ann Blandford Edwards (1831–92) visited Egypt in the winter of 1873–74 and became fascinated by its ancient civilization. The account of her travels, *A Thousand Miles up the Nile* (1877), did much to popularize Nile tourism. Concerned at the destruction and looting of archaeological sites, she founded the Egypt Exploration Fund (now Society) in 1882 to carry out and publish scientific excavations throughout Egypt. She also established the first professorship in Egyptian archaeology in England, at University College London.

We get to Wadi Halfa the end of our journey this evening and I shall then post this letter. I have not heard from you for some days as there has been no post boat and I don't expect I shall get a letter for a few days. Tell Violet that the Xmas tree is still standing on deck. The presents which we all had on Xmas eve did not come off the tree so there are still a lot of funny things to be given away. I forgot to tell you that Lady G. gave me an emerald Japanese ashtray. I shall be so glad to get home to you dearest and the children. I expect [I] shall find the return journey [a] very long one. As I leave on Feb. 3rd Monday you will be able to write to me more than once and as long as you put c/o Thomas Cook and Son Cairo Egypt I shall get it, but I don't know whether it should get [to] me in time if addressed to the P&O SS *Mongolia*, Port Said. You might write to Marseilles and also perhaps Gibraltar but I will try and let you know about that later

I shall send this now and if possible add a few lines at Wadi Halfa before posting it.

Much love dearest
Ever your loving husband
Ferdy
A.F.R. Platt

Violet xxxxxx
Rowly xxxxxxxx

Wadi Halfa
Friday Jan. 3rd 10 am

When we arrived yesterday afternoon we found there was no mail out until
10 pm tonight so I am just adding a few more lines before posting this.
Tomorrow we are going across the river to see a temple and then on donkeys to the Rock of Abusir, from the top of which you get a good view of
the 2nd Cataract. I am sending you some post cards by this mail. You will
notice that the stamps are Soudanese, as Wadi Halfa is in the Soudan. On
all the public buildings which however are not numerous the British as well
as the Egyptian flag is flying. The place is small but kept very clean. British
cleanliness! Before we were allowed to moor yesterday a quarantine officer
came aboard and examined all our crew in case we might introduce plague.
There are some cases down in the Delta but about a hundred miles from
Cairo where we came from. However it shows they are wisely strict. There
is nothing much to see here in Halfa itself. The native shops have nothing
very attractive, mostly provision.

12.15 pm – I have just come in from a short walk and donkey ride with
Sir C. . . . You won't get this for some time because the boat which will
take it tonight will be too late for the Brindisi Mail, which leaves Egypt on
Sunday. However the letter which I posted at Korosko ought to reach you
by that mail.

   I find I cannot do anything about booking a berth on the *Mongolia* here.
I must write or telegraph to Assuan. This of course makes no difference to
my plans. I am longing to get your letters. Patience!

Goodbye darling, I will write again before we leave Wadi Halfa.

Always your loving husband
Ferdy
A.F.R. Platt

Downstream from Wadi Halfa

Ferdy and his companions set out on the return journey to Cairo on Sunday, January 5, 1908; they had been on the Nile for very nearly two months. Ferdy, for one, was overjoyed to be on his way home, although he still looked forward to visiting some of the sites they had missed on their way upstream. Three days later, and exactly a month after their last visit, they arrived at Aswan, where more adventures awaited. Tea at the Savoy, and a meeting with the legendary professor Archibald Sayce, made this second stay equally memorable. But the schedules of the steamships from Port Said back to Europe would not wait, and the party rested only a few days in Aswan.

By January 15, they were back in Luxor, this time for a ten-day sojourn. This gave Ferdy plenty of opportunities to do what he liked best—leaving behind the other members of the Duke's party, striking out on his own across the desert to visit ancient sites and meet their plucky excavators. A highlight of the trip was Ferdy's meeting with Howard Carter—then unemployed (having been sacked from the Antiquities Service), impecunious, and eking out a living by painting watercolors for the tourist market. Little could Carter have imagined that, fourteen years later, he would be the most famous archaeologist in the world, following his discovery of the tomb of Tutankhamun. But that was all still in the future. In January 1908, Ferdy, the amateur Egyptolo-gist, was invited to lunch with Carter in his house near the Valley of the Kings. Ferdy also took the opportunity to climb the Theban hills behind Deir el-Bahri, glorying in the view and the atmosphere of antiquity.

Leaving the tombs of ancient Egypt's kings and queens behind, the *Serapis* continued its journey northward on Sunday, January 26, calling only at Abydos, before arriving back at the port of Cairo on Saturday, February 1. There, Ferdy and his companions disembarked their floating home of the past three months and set off into the city. Tea at Shepheard's Hotel was de rigueur for any British visitor to Egypt in those heady days of empire; but for Ferdy a visit to the Egyptian Museum was the undoubted highlight, even if he could only really scratch the surface of the building's immense collection of antiquities. By now, not even the wonders of Egypt's ancient civilization could detain Ferdy much longer in the land of the pharaohs. Home was calling.

On Monday, February 3, Ferdy departed Cairo for Port Said, and the following day his ship, the SS *Mongolia*, set sail for Marseilles, Gibraltar, and England. Ferdy waved goodbye to Egypt, never to return. Eleven days later, on Saturday, February 15, 1908, he stepped ashore in Southampton, caught a train up to London, and walked back through his front door at number 18 Hall Road, Maida Vale, London W1.

SS *Serapis* between Wadi Halfa and Abu Simbel
9.40 am Monday Jan. 6th 1908

My dearest,

Here I am on the way back to Assuan and <u>Home</u>! It is most disappointing we
have received no letters since we left Assuan. It appears that they have not
forwarded any as they did not know how long we should be at W. Halfa and
as the government boats won't stop to hand over letters (as Cooks do) they
have kept them. So I hope to find one if not two or three letters from you
dear which I am most impatient to read. I expect you will have received one
letter from me from Korosko (posted there) and one letter and some cards
from W. Halfa. I believe we missed one mail boat which passed us on its way
down to Assuan so that I could not post anything to you till the next mail.

We arrived at Wadi Halfa in the afternoon of Thursday Jan. 2nd. I went
for a short walk with Ld G. and Sir C. about the town. Next morning, Friday,
Sir C. and I went for a donkey ride into the desert, but as we had no stirrups
and wide saddles which kept your legs wide apart we could not stand it and
came back and walked about instead. In the afternoon I walked out into the
desert. I had to walk for about 20 minutes across sand to the foot of the hills.
All the offal and blood and skin, etc. of the animals killed are thrown out
into the desert and there is also a place where they seem to burn some of it. I
was walking East and the North wind blew the most horrible smell you can
imagine. However it didn't last long. I went up to the top of a hill and had a
fine view of the desert country; while I was up there I saw a jackal. You can
see for miles. The hills are not so continuous as they are in Egypt but broken
up into isolated pyramid-shaped heights which seem to rise like islands out
of a sea of sand. They are all sandstone. Sometimes they look like great ant
heaps or sugar loaves. I watched the sun set and then went home.

On Saturday Jan. 4th we went up in the *Serapis* as far as possible and then
rode on donkeys to the Rock of Abusir. Her Grace was carried in a chair by
four men. It took us about an hour to get there and then we climbed to the
top, which must be 150 feet high, and looked down upon the 2nd Cataract,
beyond which we could see the telegraph poles stretching away for miles
in the sand and beyond them the desert hills. The railway runs through the

desert 230 miles to Abu Hamed, and crossing the great loop in the Nile. The
view was very fine. The Rock is really part of a cliff, the highest part, and i
rises almost perpendicularly out of the swirling water.

We then rode back to the *Serapis* and had lunch. On our way back tc
Wadi Halfa we stopped and the D. and I went on shore to see a temple buil
in the time of Thothmes III.[1] It is quite small and in ruins but as it was fillec
up with sand and only excavated in recent years the paint on what sculpture
remains is very fresh. The Gosfords did some photography and then we wen
back to W. Halfa. As soon as we arrived, about 4.30 pm, I went off for ;
walk into the desert and got up a hill in time to see the sun set. I came home
another way north of that stink! Following the camel track in the sand. It i
very quiet in the desert and you could hear the people calling to each othe
in the town and the mueddin [muezzin] in the mosque calling the faithfu
to prayer although it was a mile or more away. As the dark red skyline grew
duller in the west I reached the town and got onto the riverfront. The street
were almost deserted and there was not such a hum of voices. I stood on the
front for a while watching the scene. A wedge of dull yellow river with dar
black banks and point of the wedge to the left, a thick lebbek tree[2] in th
foreground overhung the river, a dark red streak of sky above in the blue
Venus very bright and silvery, while below silhouetted against the sky wa
the *Serapis*' funnel, and still lower the electric lamps dotted about. The same
night we had the Mudir of Assuan (Capt. Moraut. Dur dined with us; he
came in uniform and medals).[3]

He has several prisoners, some of the Mahdi's emirs and a prophet who
would stir up mischief if he was allowed to go. One [of] these people com
plained that he hadn't enough to eat but he is allowed £3.10 a month by [the
government, which means quite enough for a man who only lives on doura.
The King of Fashoda was also there. He has one wife with him, the remain
ing twenty-something being regarded in the light of State Property were
after his deposition handed over to his nephew and successor.

I am delighted to say that since I wrote the previous pages . . . a boat came
up bringing the mail and your two very welcome letters and paper. It seemec

---

1   Thutmose III, fifth king of the Eighteenth Dynasty (reigned c. 1479–1425 BC).
2   The lebbek tree *(Albizia lebbeck)*, grown as forage, and also for its timber and medicinal
     properties.
3   In this context, the *mudir* is the term for headman.
4   A type of sorghum.

ages since I had had any news. I dare say I shall get some more before we reach Assuan. The two I have were posted on the 25–27th Dec. I am glad to get all the news to know you are well and that things are going on alright.

You will see from this that I have come to the end of my Medieval Cream wove bank writing tablet and have to fall back on the other paper. It will help you to know in referring to my letters when I began the return voyage down the Nile. We are now nearing Korosko and I hope to get a walk before and during sunset. The Duke and party get a great number of letters; Sir C. gets very few. I am so glad you spent a happy Xmas Day. I expect you enjoyed it a good deal more than I did in spite of the good things we had. For you could talk to people you cared for and who care for you, whereas I was in the midst of civil indifference and no one to care for. I think I told you how I silently drank to you all, also on New Years' Eve and Day. Now you have that brass fine screen you won't make your dear little face like a boiled lobster any more but it won't stop you from toasting your equally dear little legs I expect! Poor Miss "Trefusis": I was afraid she would not go on long at that game. What a pity it is that she doesn't give it all up. Mrs Reynolds must be worried over her sister. It doesn't sound very satisfactory. Remember me to her and the rest of them. Also Mrs Druce. I wonder what the end of the case will be . . . I shall stop now – I don't think it will be any good posting till we get to Assuan or till a post boat catches us up, but I shall shut this up and stamp it on the chance of it being posted at Korosko.

5.25 pm – We have passed Korosko and are evidently going on until it is dark. However I shall say good bye and seal it up on the chance.

Much love darling. I am longing to look into your dear eyes again.

Your always loving husband
Ferdy
A.F.R. Platt

Violet
xxxxxxxx

Boy
xxxxxxx

SS *Serapis* Korosko
10.45 am Tuesday Jan. 7th 1908

My dearest,

This is practically a continuation of yesterday's and will go by the same
mail when we get to Shellal tonight. I forgot to tell you that we waited
on Sunday at Wadi Halfa until three o'clock waiting for the letters which
never came. So instead of getting to Abu Simbel and anchoring for the
night we had to do so farther up the river and when we came to the temple
we had to pass it although we slowed down for a bit while Lady Theo. took
a photo of it. The "Prince Abbas" (Cook's tourist steamer) brought them
up with them. Both steamers whistled and stopped and we sent a boat of
to get the mail and other things as well. This morning we took on board
from another of Cooks boats meat, live fowls and a turkey, bread, fruit, etc

Before we left Wadi Halfa I went for three hours' walk in the desert
leaving before 9 am and getting back soon after 12. It was a different walk
to any I had been [on] before. It was easy to lose the way and I had to make
use of landmarks in the shape of stones piled up by people who had been
there before. After crossing the level sand I went up a narrow sandy valley
between two hills which became narrower and steeper as I neared the top
and finally I found myself on a plateau with more hills rising from it and
so on. There was a fine valley winding along with high walls of rock and
walked along the edge looking down into it. Whilst doing so I suddenly saw
a huge hyena with a very bushy tail; he quickly made his way down into the
valley below and galloped away for several hundred yards till he got out o
sight up a side valley. Sir C. has his gun with him (but nothing will induce
him to take exercise although he is always talking about it; he eats too much
and has become very fat) and he might have shot this hyena easily. When
there is very little wind in the desert, the silence is so absolute that you can
hear your watch tick and the throbbing of the arteries in your head. This
absolute silence in the desert is very strange and uncanny. Even the very
air seems dead when there is no wind. If you throw a stone or clap your
hands there may be one or several echoes, but they end so suddenly and the
subsequent silence is so intense that even the sound appeared to be killed

– struck dead in the midst of the surrounding lifelessness. From all this you might think that the desert must be very unattractive, even forbidding, but to me it certainly is not, though I dare say it would be to some extent if the sky were overcast with dark clouds.

As it is, the brilliant sun, clear sky, the warm yellows, browns and purples of the sand and sandstones, the ever changing hills, gorges and plateaus which succeed one another in the course of a two hours' walk make the desert most fascinating. It is full of topographical surprises. As you walk along a more or less level plateau between hills, you suddenly find yourself on the edge of a deep winding ravine, and to get to the other side you must either clamber down the rocky side, cross the intervening sand and climb the opposite wall or else walk along until you come to the end of the valley and can walk round it. This means that you have to be careful in attempting short cuts in the wrong direction and noting all your landmarks. I fear my letters must be as barren as the desert of which they are so full and you must be tired of hearing about the wilderness. But I have some excuse, I think, for I have been driven out into it by a combination of circumstances, amongst which I may mention want of congenial occupation (temples, etc.) and exercise. So I have spent a good deal of time there. And you can't imagine how much I enjoy it, not only the scenery but the rest to ear and eye.

It is a pleasure to get away from the monotonous noise of the machinery on board, whether of the paddles or the electric light, but just think how I sit there and revel in the absence of motor bus, cabs, traction engines, railways, whistles and all the other noises of that pandemonium called London. There is one drawback to walking in the desert. It is absolute ruination to one's boots. The leather all dries up and the rough sandstone cuts through the stitches.

We have just finished lunch and I am writing this in my cabin. Doors and windows are all open as the thermometer stands at 80°F. As I look out of the door or the window next to it I see villages, palm trees, sakkiehs [waterwheels] and the river in front with a background of sandstone hills and yellow sand which lies in most graceful curves, bright green patches of "Bursim", Castor oil bushes, lebbek or acacia trees and doum palms[1] – all lend variety to the scene. From the opposite window my view is curtailed by the week's wash on two lines. We are spinning along at a good pace as we

---

1   Native African tree bearing a fruit with the taste of gingerbread.

are going with the stream and as we are not stopping in the middle of the day anywhere to see sights we shall get to – I no sooner wrote these words then the boat stopped and I find we are going to land and have a look at the Temple of Gerf Hosseyn.[1]

3.30 – Just come back from the temple, which is something like Abu Simbel (on a smaller scale) inside being cut out of the rock. It has in front the remains of a small hall of columns. It is of the time of Rameses II but the work is not at all equal to the best of that period. On the way back we witnessed an amusing row between some [of] our crew and the natives. The former only speak Arabic while the latter, being Nubians, talks a Barber [Berber] language only. One of our men wanted to get some eggs, which are cheaper here than at Assuan. Now the Arabic word for egg is bade or "bed", but in Nubian it is a bad word (the meaning of which I will tell you when I come home). So they thought they were being insulted. However the dragoman put an end to the row by explaining to them what they wanted. The fresh eggs we get here make capital omelettes but they are very small. I have nothing but toast and coffee for breakfast as I find I am better without anything else. Even when I walk 3 hours in the desert! I never seem to get tired there! I shall be so glad to taste really good milk, tea, coffee and bread once more. I ought not to grumble about the coffee, as Lady G. had some and a special coffee pot from that shop Picard's in Regent St. But as it is black coffee I don't care for it so much. It is all finished now so we are using the ordinary coffee, which is also good.

The things on the Xmas tree were never distributed but this morning Lord G. told me to get a pair of scissors and help myself so I have cut off a few things for the children. This cabin of mine is 85°F at 4.15 with door and windows open; last night it was very warm and we did not have the sail cloth put down all round the boat and could sit out after dinner without feeling chilly.

This morning Lord G. came up and called me at 4.30 am to see the Southern Cross which I saw for the first time. It was more like a cross than I expected. The young moon looked very pretty the night before last with Venus a little above it and in the same straight vertical line. I don't think there is any more to tell you at present but if there is I will add it if possible

---

1   Temple on the west bank of the Nile built by the viceroy of Nubia, Setau, during the second half of the reign of Ramesses II (c. 1245–1230 BC). Following the construction of the Aswan High Dam, the temple was entirely submerged under the waters of Lake Nasser.

before posting this and yesterday's letter at Shellal. We are nearing the Tropic of Cancer.

Much love dearest from
Your ever loving husband
Ferdy
A.F.R. Platt

SS *Serapis*, Assuan
6 pm Wednesday Jan. 8th 1908

My dearest,

This is the third letter which you ought to get by this mail. My anticipation about the time of our arrival was all wrong, as we had much further to go than I thought, and it took longer than they said. Consequently we had to tie up last night at the beginning of that picturesque gorge of rocky scenery near Kalabsheh. As we did not start till 10 o'clock this morning we were able to see it again in the morning light.

When we reached the locks of the dam, I got off the boat and walked across the dam itself. On the way I met McCorquodale and then returned . . . I was going to walk to Assuan while the boat went through the locks and steamed down the Cataract. He very kindly sent his servant to show me the best way to go, which was not the same as that by which I went to Shellal . . . When I left the boat I started to walk soon after 2; I found it extremely hot. I was wet through by the time I had gone half-way but after a rest in the shade and sitting in the sun and the breeze I dried up again. For about the first hour I was quite sheltered from the wind, which was more east than north and the sun on my back, which made it very trying but it was delightful when I reached the top of the hills looking over the Cataract. I saw the *Serapis* below me winding in and out among the rocks. It takes a long time to get through the four locks; she only just fits there and they take about 20 minutes to fill. So she did not catch me up until I [had finished] more than ¾ of the walk. I could also see the Ibis, Ld. G's boat following slowly

down. The G.s got on board it as soon as they passed the last lock. The
took their tea with them and I saw them moor on the opposite bank (west
in the shade to have it. I walked on and had the luxury of tea and sunse
on the verandah of the Cataract Hotel. I had a most appalling thirst whe
I arrived and before I had any tea I went to the American Bar and had
"John Collins", i.e. ice, soda water, fresh lime juice, a little sugar and a littl
gin. That is the only one of those fancy American drinks worth drinking i
my opinion. I was introduced to it in Peterboro' years ago. You can't imag
ine what a thirst you get when it is <u>really</u> hot in the desert and how joll
good that sort of acid drink is. I am not a thirsty subject as a rule and afte
all my other desert walks I never felt <u>very</u> thirsty but I did today! After te
I took a boat from the hotel and rowed to the *Serapis* . . . at her old plac
again on the east bank of the Island of Elephantine opposite Assuan no
very far from the temple which you can see in the photos. . . .

I am waiting for your next letter which will tell me your opinion about m
coming by long sea. I shall then make arrangements to book a berth on th
Mongolia.

8.30 am Thursday Jan. 9th 1908

Yesterday was one of the hottest if not <u>the</u> hottest day we have had. Eve
the dragoman complained. There was very little wind and what there wa
came from the N.E. across the desert and consequently was very hot. I hav
just finished my breakfast and am going to the hotel to get my hair cut an
then go for a walk in the desert. I believe we stay here some days, certainl
to Saturday. As we go downstream we shall meet the post instead of goin
further and further away, so I shall get your letters sooner. The *Serap*
looks very queer this morning. The awning which covers the deck from
end to end has become perfectly black from the smuts from the funne
especially since we left Wadi Halfa and faced the N. wind which carrie
them all behind, so they have taken it all down and are going to put up
clean one I suppose – the *Serapis* looks very bare and naked.
   Last night it was so hot that they played bridge on deck instead of [in
the cabin. The night before Sir C. felt quite bad and couldn't sleep owin
to the heat in that stuffy little cabin. So did Lady G. Old people don't min
heat at all, nor foul air apparently.

The box that Ferdy painted for his daughter Violet in 1913, in which were kept his letters from his Nile journey.

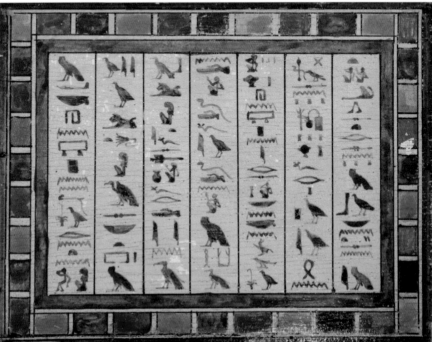

The two ends of the box on which Ferdy painted his hieroglyphic messages.

TEL. PADDINGTON 2245.

18, HALL ROAD,
N.W.8.

Inscriptions on the Egyptian box which I painted for Violet

Translation.

A.

Year 13 month 8 day 30 under the majesty of George, fifth of that name –
Says the physician Ferdinand. "Behold I have painted this box with my own hand for my daughter whom I love, Violet.
I did this in order that my memory may remain firm in the heart of my daughter and that my name may be in her mouth"

B.

Behold this box belongs to the maiden Violet
Her Mother was the Mistress of the house Mabel; her father the Physician Ferdinand.
He says" I have spoken with words of magical power over this box
If any one injures it or damages the writing upon it, my curse shall reach them wherever they may be

Ferdy's own translations of his hieroglyphs, which were kept in the box. Translation A is of the end above and translation B is of the end below, opposite.

Samuel Platt, Ferdy's grandfather, in the uniform of a Deputy Lieutenant of Middlesex.

Colonel Charles Rowley Platt, Ferdy's father, in the uniform of a Military Knight of Windsor.

Ernest Rowley Platt, Ferdy's brother, when at the Royal Military College, Sandhurst, in 1885.

Ferdy Platt on entering Eton in 1876.

Ferdy as a young medical student
at Edinburgh University.

Ferdy with his brother Ernest, at about
the time of his first visit to Egypt in 1896.

Dr Ferdinand Platt at home in London, at 18 Hall Road NW8, where he also had his consulting room. He is with his wife May and her sister Lily.

Ferdy's daughter Violet, circa 1903.

Ferdy's son Rowley about the time of the voyage.

Ernest with the band of the regiment he later commanded in Quetta, then in India. Ferdy mused that it was "odd that Erny had met [Churchill] in the Kyber Pass 10 years ago and now I have met him at the 1st Cataract."

Rowley Platt as a settler in Subukia in the Kenyan Rift Valley in the 1930s. Ferdy visited him there and painted views from his farm.

A photograph taken by Ferdy of his daughter Violet accompanying his brother Ernest and nephew John on a family shooting party in 1930. The dog-owner in the middle is Ernest's brother-in-law, Bertie Innes-Hopkins.

A benign Dr. Ferdinand Platt in retirement in his Kent country home.

A sculpture of Mabel Platt, signed and dated by Herbert Hampton in 1911. Ferdy in 1908 asks several times for news of its progress. Hampton was renowned for his public statues, which ironically were to include the 8th Duke of Devonshire's monument in Whitehall.

Ferdy's secretaire, which housed his favorite books and everyday possessions. His fondness for it is attested by the two watercolors (opposite) of a vase of peonies and his pipe stand, which he painted using it as the background.

Intimate still lives painted
by Ferdy.

1

S.S. "Serapis" anchored at Bedreshein 15 miles from Cairo
6.30 P.M Thursday Nov. 7th 1907

My dearest May,

We left our moorings this afternoon beside the Rameses at 2.45 and although I finished a letter and posted it before we started I am beginning another this evening so as to keep abreast of events. The Gosfords & Sir C. H. went into Cairo this morning but I did not feel inclined so stayed on board. Lady Theo. also as she was ill – I saw her after breakfast and again this evening. She ate something which disagreed with her. The Rameses "next door" was being got ready to start next Tuesday and the men were cleaning the deck. Natives with bare feet. Each man had a bundle of some sort of things under his right foot. The deck was wet & sprinkled with sand or holystone. One man in front began to sing a few words & then the rest joined in chorus. As they did so each man worked his right foot up along the deck then brought his left across to his right then right foot down. In this way they gradually moved along the deck in unison. I was very glad when we started as we were quite shut in all round with canvas which not only kept off the sun & prevented people looking in but it kept out the wind & prevented one getting any view, and what is worse kept in the mosquitoes & midges. We have been horribly bitten & the irritation is disagreeable any one is scratching & putting on all sorts of things.

This afternoon we started in rather cloudy weather but with a

---

The long journey on the Nile begins with the first of Ferdy's letters, which his wife was to preserve, dated 6.30 pm on Thursday November 7, 1907, from the SS *Serapis* anchored at Bedreshein, fifteen miles from Cairo.

P&O S.S. "Mongolia"

Marseilles

Saturday Feb. 8th 1908

My dearest, I have no particular news since I posted my letter last night except the following — I received your letter this morning also one from Evvy and Lily. The ship does not leave till 10. AM tomorrow morning, and as we arrived about 9 AM (owing to mist this morning) that is more than 24 hours. So I have had plenty of time to read your letter I did not receive any letter from

The last letter in the collection, from aboard the SS *Mongolia* on the homeward journey in Marseilles, dated Saturday February 8, 1908.

When Ferdy took the Duke of Devonshire to meet Howard Carter, the ultimately famous archaeologist was at a low point in his career and making a living as an accomplished watercolorist. The Duke bought two pictures, which may have been similar to the above, titled *Under the Protection of the Gods*, which Carter painted in 1908, the year of the meeting.

Common swallow and Egyptian swallow, by Charles Whymper.

Coot on the Sacred Lake at Karnak, by Charles Whymper. Ferdy became a friend of Whymper, whom he met several times. Whymper was working on these watercolors, which were among those published in *Egyptian Birds*, in 1909.

Two contemporary views of the SS *Serapis* on the Nile.

No more news at present. I am reading *Kipps* by H.G. Wells and like it as far as I have read.

I have read several other indifferent novels the names and plots of which have gone out of my head. One was *Ancestors*, another *The Fighting Chance* by Robert Chambers (an American book).

Much love darling to you and the chicks and to all at No. 10.

Always your devoted and loving husband
Ferdy
A.F.R. Platt

Violet
xxx
xxxx

Boy
xxx
xxxx
xx

SS *Serapis* Assuan
Sat. Jan. 11th 1908

My dearest,

Just a few hurried lines to tell you that I received your two letters and the newspapers and to say that I have told Cook to engage my berth on the *Mongolia*. Thank dear little Violet for her nice letter. I had a very stiff and lugubrious letter from Sunny Jim, who is as you said depressed about his practice. After two hot days we had a desert storm yesterday.

The day before yesterday it was 90°F in the dining room and 89°F in my cabin. It was cloudy and oppressive. I had a walk in the desert and I simply was dripping. I walked about with my coat and waistcoat off.

Everyone felt it and the D., etc. played bridge on deck in the evening.
Yesterday I went out with L.G. and Sir C. to get tobacco, etc. and I had a
short walk in the desert. It was too dusty to walk in certain places. In the
afternoon I walked down the riverfront but the dust blowing across the
river was trying. I went to the Savoy and had tea with Sir S. MacKenzie.

Just going over to catch post; will write again later.

Much love from
Your ever loving husband
Ferdy

SS *Serapis*, Assuan, Egypt
Sunday Jan. 12th 1908 10.45 am

My dearest,

I am writing this in the desert to the East of Assuan out of sight of the
town and river. I am lying on a big bank of sand, sheltered from the hot
sun by a huge overhanging granite rock. I can hear nothing but the rustle
of the breeze, the buzzing of one or two thin flies, the feeble twittering
of a couple of little sand-coloured birds about the size of a very thin spar-
row and the occasional sound of a distant railway whistle. All round me
are small hills and valleys, tumbled granite boulders and sand – sand in
quantities which would have made the Walrus and the Carpenter weep.[1]
    In some places there is only a thin layer, in others there are great drifts
such as I am sitting on. The wind blows the sand into curious shapes and
covers the surface with ripples. Where I am the bank is rounded but

1   A reference to Lewis Carroll's poem "The Walrus and the Carpenter" (in *Through the
     Looking-Glass*), which includes the lines:
     The Walrus and the Carpenter
     Were walking close at hand;
     They wept like anything to see
     Such quantities of sand

farther away it runs out for more than a hundred paces into a bank about twenty feet high at the top of the ridge, which is quite sharp like the edge of a very long thick knife [drawing of sand ridge]; it is hard enough to walk along the top without sinking in very deep. But I fancy you must have heard enough about the desert.

I posted a letter to you yesterday morning in a great hurry because I was told I could catch the Brindisi Mail. So I think you will probably get four letters from me by one post. After that I went for my usual walk in the desert. In the afternoon Lady G. asked me to go with them to see one of the coffins of the sacred rams opened by the French men. It was most interesting. It took some time to empty out the mixture of sand and salt before the mummy could be removed. The head was covered with a mask and pectoral all in one piece which was made of cartonnage[1] covered with gold. The pectoral was ornamented with figures of gods and on the lower border was a short inscription in hieroglyphics. Hung round its neck was a wreath of what were probably olive leaves. Lady G. was given some of them. She and Lady T. took photos of them. I then walked back to the *Serapis* while the G.s went for a sail in their boat the Ibis.

We leave for Luxor on Tuesday and I will let you know in my next if possible what my future movements are to be. Sir C. told me that he will be jolly glad to get home. He has had enough of it. So have I. Of course I enjoy these desert walks very much, and in this beautiful dry bracing air and sunshine and even on board the boat one is living practically in the open air. But as I can't visit the tombs here without spending money I can only walk, and I get rather sick of my own society. In his letter Jim tells me that his brother left for Egypt on the 31st and wonders whether I shall see him. He is going to stay at Helwan.[2] So is the Duke, but it is probable that I shall leave them at Luxor, in order to catch the boat at Port Said. They have engaged the *Serapis* up to the 5th of Feb. That is three days after I leave P.S. so they may not go to Helwan till then. I expect I shall have to stay a night in Cairo. I hope I shall be able to run into the museum before I leave as I saw very little of it before we went up the Nile.

---

1   A mummy case made of tightly fitting layers of linen or papyrus glued together.
2   Helwan, south of Cairo, was a spa resort much favored for its waters.

Monday Jan. 13th

I did not have much walk this morning as I went over with Sir C. to Cook and the bazaar. The *Mongolia* leaves on Feb. 3rd, arrives Brindisi 6th London on the 15th. I shall post a letter on board to go by the Brindisi train on the 6th; after that I am not certain whether I can post again at Marseilles or Naples or Gibraltar. However I will let you know. I think i better to come back by sea.

Tuesday Jan. 14th

I am just going across to post this. I saw Professor Sayce yesterday and had tea with him on his dahabeeyeh and showed him my paper on the origin o the name of Elephantine and told me I ought to send it up to the Sec. of the Bib. Arch. Soc. [The Society for Biblical Archaeology] I don't think there i any more news, so will close this.

Much love to you darling and the chicks
Ever your loving husband

Ferdy
A.F.R. Platt

SS *Serapis*, Luxor, Egypt
Wednesday Jan. 15th 1908

My dearest, after leaving Assuan yesterday morning we steamed to Kom Ombo and arrived just after lunch. This time we stopped at the temple and we all went ashore to see it. You will remember that on the way up I did not see it. We then went on a little lower to where we stayed before, opposite Birch' house (the manager of Cassell's Company), and they all went up to the house to tea. I stayed behind as I did not want to go and they did not ask me.

   I woke rather early this morning and got up while it was dark, thinking might have another look at the Southern Cross, but I found the sky covered

The granite rocks of Elephantine Island, Aswan

The article that Ferdy referred to in his letter of Tuesday January 14, "The Origin of the Name of the Island of Elephantine," was indeed published, along with a photographic plate, in: *Proceedings of the Society of Biblical Archaeology* XXX, no. CCXXVI (June 1908), 206–207. The author's name is given as A.F.R. Platt, M.B.

The flavor of the article can be appreciated from the opening and final paragraphs:

Two explanations of the origin of the word Elephantine are current. One is that the island (or city on it) was the centre of the ivory trade, which is not very convincing. The other is that the Egyptians first saw elephants in the neighbourhood. There are difficulties in accepting this if the elephants were wild, because the Nile Valley in Nubia or Egypt was not, in historical times, a suitable habitat for the animal which requires large tracts of forest.

There is a third possible explanation not less plausible than the other two.

At Assuan the intrusion of the granite into the sandstone breaks up the Nile into a series of rocks and rapids, extending some five miles up the river, to form what is known as the First Cataract. This granite has been split up and weathered into rounded water-worn masses, often covered with a dark grey or black shiny deposit of manganese dioxide. In many of them "pot-holes" have been scoured out when the Nile was much higher and swifter. These holes vary in depth and position, some are deep, vertical and conical, such as that near the Nilometer on Elephantine; others are lateral and often mere shallow depressions.

Some of these rocks present a curious resemblance to elephants, the general outline of the rock corresponding to that of the animal; while the proboscis, legs, tail, ears, and eyes may appear more or less clearly according to the position, number, depth, and arrangement of the shadows formed by the pot-holes and other markings, and particularly by the direction and amount of light.

[...]

I hope members of the Society may know of facts in favour of this Petrous derivation of the world Elephantine; for without confirmatory evidence this "elephant" hypothesis, like the other two, must remain as nebulous as Hamlet's camel, weasel and whale.

Ferdy's article was obviously well-received, for in the following year's volume—PSBA XXXI, no. CCXXXII (May 1909), 172–84—he published a much longer article entitled "The Ancient Egyptian Methods of Working Hard Stones," full of scholarly references. Thereafter, however, there are no further articles and Ferdy seems to have returned to his medicine!

with clouds and day breaking. However I saw a beautiful sunrise instead. It was just like two sunrises following, for all the clouds were pink at first and when that died out in a few minutes the clouds at the edge of the horizon became blood red and the real sunrise began. The sky remained cloudy all day and consequently it was rather cold facing the wind – temp. only 61 in the cabin at lunch time. We started at 8 o'clock and steamed all day at Esneh. The clouds broke and the sun shone between them, casting great shadows over the fine lofty limestone hills below Esneh, which is quite a novelty after so many weeks of sunshine. I had hoped we might have a fine sunset but the clouds were so big and black in the west that there was nothing to see. We kept on steaming long after dark in order to tie up at Luxor, which we did not reach till 7.15 this evening. I ought to have found a letter from you but they all went up to Assuan as the D. did not tell the dragoman that he wanted to get to Luxor, without stopping, from Kom Ombo. As I have told you before no one seems to know what is going to happen. It is always the same. Lord G., who is most methodical, generally predicts what will go wrong. He and the others never say anything because it would do no good.

I hope I shall get a letter tomorrow from you, but I intend to post this even if I don't, so that you will not have to wait so long for a letter, and I know you must like to get them on several days and not all in a bunch.

I find that the *Mongolia* does not go to Brindisi at all (as I wrote on the outside of my last letter) but straight to Marseilles and touches at Gibraltar, so I shall be able to post a letter the day before I leave Cairo which will go to Brindisi, and that you will get a week after I have started – and the next week instead of getting a letter you will get me! I am wondering what will be the best way to get from Liverpool [St. Station] or Fenchurch St. [Station] home. What I should like to do would be to have my luggage delivered by the railway people if they would do so in a reasonable time and come by underground to Edgware Road Station with just a bag and then get onto a bus, but I suppose I shall have to take a cab. Ask your father and let me know. There will be time to write a reply . . . I am longing to get home to see you and the children.

8.50 am Thursday Jan. 16th 1908

To my delight and surprise I received a letter from you just before my breakfast. As I breakfast before the others are up alone I was able to sit and enjoy reading it. It is the one which you wrote on 6th and 7th Jan. and which went

up to Assuan. I believe I shall get another one with the paper about 11 am.
Meanwhile I am going to walk out to Karnak.

2.30 pm
I have just finished lunch. I had a long walk at Karnak going on the top of the
enclosing wall from which there is a fine view of all the ruined temples, and
then down amongst the ruins themselves. When I came home I <u>was</u> pleased to
find another letter from you. Thank you dearest for them both, also the paper.
I did not get time to read your 2nd letter before lunch, so you can imagine how
impatient I was to get the meal over. The thing which strikes me more than
anything else in your letters is the extraordinary variety of extremes of weather
you seem to have had during the last month. It is quite bewildering. I do hope
you won't be penny wise and pound foolish in the matter of coals while the cold
lasts, which does not seem to be many days at a time. I am so sorry you have a
cold: I hope it is better. In your 2nd letter today you say the children's colds are
better but you say nothing about your own. I hope Violet has enjoyed her party
at the Wilmers. I should like to get them as patients. They seem very well off.
We are having another windy, cloudy day although there is more sun, but the
dust is blowing very much, which is not pleasant. However one can walk better
when it is cooler in Luxor. For although it was much hotter at Assuan there
was less cultivated ground and consequently less moisture. The Nile Valley at
Assuan and up to Halfa is very narrow and the desert hills are always within a
short walk and in some places the sandstone hills become limestone at Gebel
Abu Feda, comes down to the water's edge. Here the eastern hills are miles
away from the river and the cultivated land extends a long way inland. I believe
I shall see a good deal more here before I leave as they are going to stay here
until they go to Helwan, which is about 15 miles from Cairo opposite Sakkara.
I shall stay here until the end of the month I expect, and then stay a night or
two in Cairo. But I will write again and tell you what my movements are. As
long as you put c/o Thomas Cook & Son Cairo, I shall get all letters because I
shall let them know when I am going to leave the *Serapis*. The railway journey
to Cairo lasts from the afternoon of one day to the following morning.

Much love darling from
your always loving husband
Ferdy
(A.F.R. Platt)

SS *Serapis* Luxor
Jan. 18th 1908

My dearest,

I am afraid there is not much news for you. I have been over the temple
of Luxor twice and Karnak twice but it would not interest you to enter
into archaeological details. Some jewelry has been found by Mr. Ayrton
working for Mr. Theodore Davis, a rich American who has for some years
[been] paying the expenses of digging in the Valley of the Tombs of the
Kings. The Duke and the rest are to go on board Davis' Dahabayeh this
morning to see the jewelry, and if I am asked I suppose I shall go too.
met Whymper this morning, who has asked me to go and see him on a
Dahabayeh which has been lent to him. Like me he has been without
anyone to talk to but only for a fortnight! Think of me for nearly 2½

Edward Ayrton and Theodore Davis

Theodore Davis

Having first excavated for Flinders Petrie, Edward
Russell Ayrton (1882–1914) worked as an
archaeologist for American lawyer and archaeological sponsor Theodore Davis (1838–1915)
in the Valley of the Kings from 1905 to 1908. He
left Egypt in 1911 to take up an appointment in
the Archaeological Survey of Ceylon, where he
drowned only three years later while on a shooting expedition.

   With other members of the Gilded Age,
Davis spent his summers in Newport, Rhode
Island, but his winters he spent on a *dahabiya*
on the Nile, with his companion Mrs. Emma
Andrews. Having developed a keen interest in Egyptology and in 1902 Davis
obtained a permit from the Egyptian government to dig in the Valley of the Kings,
employing first Howard Carter, then Edward Ayrton to carry out excavations. In
1914, after several lackluster seasons, Davis relinquished the concession, declaring
"the Valley of the Tombs is now exhausted." Eight years later, it yielded the greatest
archaeological treasure of all time, the intact tomb of Tutankhamun.

months! You will remember that we saw him over at Deir el Bahri, and that he is an artist and the brother of the Alpine Climber.

I am longing to get home. I am so sick of being so sick of being so much alone and yet not able to do what I like. Nothing on earth would enduce me to go again with people like this unless I knew them first or knew what they were like. It is deadly dull at meals. It is so odd that if I am alone with anyone of the party they will talk to me but at meals, never, except to ask me a question about some scientific subject. In fact I feel that I am "kept in my place". I curse when they talk about their friends, etc. I am not expected to take part in the conversation but even when it is general talk I am never spoken to. If I could have left on the 24th I would have done so but . . . I can't see anything at all suitable. At Assuan I bought a necklace of pink quartz for Violet but Boy is so young and being a boy there seems to be nothing here he would care for. There are no toys. I got a doll for V. but I can't give him a doll. However I shall try again, at Cairo if I can't get anything here. I may get something at Gibraltar. I hope your cold is better now and that you will say so in your next letter. This is the last letter I shall write to which you can reply unless you write to Marseilles or Gibraltar.

I intend to spend a few shillings in going over to the other side of the river to the Valley of the Tombs of the Kings to see Ayrton also to see some other tombs there. I have no desert to walk in here and I can't stop on board all day. I expect I shall have more to tell you in my next letter but I know you would rather have a short letter than none at all. It was very cold last night and at 8.30 the temp. in the dining room was only 44°F, but now it is 65°. Give Violet and boy a big bear's hug for me and tell them that Daddy is longing to see them and have a romp. Thank Violet for her pot hooks, etc.; she is improving.

Much love darling
Ever your devoted loving husband
Ferdy
A.F.R. Platt

Sir Eldon and Lady Gorst came on board last evening to call on the D. and Lady T. went back to dine with them on their boat.

Sir Eldon Gorst

Sir Eldon Gorst (1861–1911), British consul-general in Egypt 1907–11, was a career diplomat, educated at Eton and Cambridge, who specialized in Egyptian affairs. After replacing Lord Cromer as consul-general, he trod a delicate path between the politicians in London and the nationalists in Egypt—before being struck down with cancer at an early age.

Sketch of Sir Eldon Gorst
by Sir Francis Carruthers Gould

SS *Serapis*, Luxor
Wednesday Jan. 22nd 1908

My dearest, I was glad to hear all your news in your letter received yesterday but you don't say how your cold is, so I suppose you are well again. You have had most extraordinary weather in England. I find it difficult to form a connected idea of what goes on in England for two reasons: it takes a week for a letter to arrive, but the Duke gets a bundle of press telegrams and I hear little scraps before I see the weekly *Times* and . . . the weather [ ] get hopelessly mixed up with telegrams, your letters and newspapers. I was anxious [to] know how Violet enjoyed the Wilmers' party. She must have looked a dear little soul in the dress you made her. I was sorry she missed the Davis party. I shall be glad to [see] you and the children again. I almost regret having arranged to come home by long sea; still I think it best for me as I should feel the cold so much and I do hate railway travelling, especially at night. I am sorry I can't go down to Cairo by boat as I must travel at night. Leaving Luxor at 6.30 and arriving at 8am next morning. I shall stay a night or two in Cairo as I do want to see the Museum. It was a great disappointment that I could not do so before we left Mena House. The Duke was so bad that I did not like to be out of the way.

Did I tell you that I was hailed by Whymper the artist just as I was going on board the other day? He is sharing a dahabayeh belonging to another artist named Nicol. On Sunday I went there to have a chat as W[hymper] hadn't talked to anyone for a fortnight, so we were both glad of the chance. I met Howard Carter there. I met him at Deir El Bahri when I was in Egypt before; he [was] an artist and quite a young fellow in those days. He was copying the paintings in the temple of Queen Hatshepsut at Deir El Bahri. Some time after that he was made Inspector of Antiquities. Two years ago he had a row with some French tourists and although he was exonerated he was asked to write a letter saying he was sorry it had happened but he declined and had to resign. He has now gone back to painting. He asked me over to lunch with him on Monday. I went over early and climbed to the top of the mountain at the back and to the left of Deir El Bahri. It is much higher than the cliff [over]looking Deir El Bahri and although a very stiff climb it well repaid the trouble, as the view from the top was magnificent. It took more than an hour to get to the top (not counting rowing across) and the donkey ride to Carter's

Charles Whymper

Whymper's watercolor of a lapwing

Charles Whymper (1853–1941) was a British artist who provided illustrations for books on travel, sport, and natural history, including *Birds of Egypt*, published in 1909. He was the brother of the Alpine mountaineer Edward Whymper, who made the controversial first ascent of the Matterhorn in 1865, in which four of his party were killed. Charles and Edward were the sons of Josiah Whymper, a renowned wood engraver and illustrator.

house which really belongs to the Government. It was erected for the use of the Service of Antiquities but as it was not wanted this year Maspero gave him permission to live in it. I had lunch with him and Nicol the artist who is staying there for a time with Carter while Whymper is on his boat. Carter has done some very beautiful work. What he does is to copy some of the best Egyptian figures or scenes very accurately as to the matter of outline and general colour. He leaves out all the cracks and damage and restores what is left. But the great charm is that he shades the colours to make it look real; for instance the golden vulture head dress of a queen he has shaded in such a way that without altering the drawing in the least it looks like real gold. I will tell you more about it when I get home.

Howard Carter

Carter with the sarcophagus of Tutankhamun

Howard Carter (1874–1939), British Egyptologist, was co-discoverer, with Lord Carnarvon, of the tomb of Tutankhamun, in 1922. Fourteen years earlier, at the time of Ferdy's meeting, Carter's fortunes were at an all-time low. Carter was as irascible as he was brilliant, and prone to making enemies. After a particularly heated altercation with some French tourists, Carter had refused to apologize and was promptly sacked as chief inspector of antiquities by the Egyptian Antiquities Service, then under French control. So when Ferdy encountered Carter at Thebes, he had fallen back on his old talents and was eking out a living as a watercolorist, producing pretty paintings of ancient Egyptian monuments to sell to tourists. (At Ferdy's urging, the Duke of Devonshire bought a couple, but they were beyond Ferdy's limited budget.) Nobody could have imagined the change in fortune that lay ahead for Carter in the Valley of the Kings—a destiny forged that very season, when Carter was first introduced to the Earl of Carnarvon on the banks of the Nile in Luxor.

Gaston Maspero

Maspero unwraps a mummy in the Boulak Museum in Cairo

A brilliant scholar, French Egyptologist Gaston Camille Charles Maspero (1846–1916) succeeded François Mariette as director of the Antiquities Service, introducing properly regulated excavations throughout Egypt, and director of the Egyptian Museum in Cairo, where he arranged and catalogued the collections. He also inaugurated the systematic clearance and preservation of the temples of Karnak. His published works exceed in number those of any other Egyptologist.

After lunch I went with Carter to the Tombs of the Queens and saw the tomb of Queen Nefert-Ari, the wife of Rameses II. She is the queen I have just mentioned and it was in this tomb he copied the painting of her. She was a beautiful woman and Carter's painting brings this out in a wonderful way. I have never before seen pictures of anything Egyptian that I have really longed to buy and possess. If I had the money spare I would buy this particular picture without a moment's hesitation. As you can imagine Carter's loss of his appointment is a serious thing for him, and he was and is I believe very hard up. I told the Duke about him and he has asked me to go over to Medinet Habu[1] with him to see Carter's sketches as he wants to help him by buying some. I am very glad to have been the means of doing this. I wish I could buy some myself. He has done a sweet little piece of one of those fowling scenes like the one in my consulting room. It represents the little daughter who is not sitting between her father's feet as in mine but standing on the back of the green punt and holding against her breast a little nestling bird. It is beautiful.

---

1   Archaeological site on the west bank of the Nile at Luxor, dominated by the well-preserved mortuary temple of the Twentieth Dynasty pharaoh Ramesses III (c. 1160 BC).

The tombs which I saw in the Valley of the Tombs of the Queens are quite new to me as they have been opened since I was in Egypt last. Some of them are in an excellent state of preservation and the colours quite fresh. Some of the blues are very vivid. Nefert-Ari's tomb is very big and the work fine considering that it is XIX Dynasty. I enjoyed the day very much and did not get home till long after sunset. I was at Karnak yesterday afternoon. The Dr. on the *Rameses* which is here now called on me and asked me to dine with him on board tonight. His name is Jackman and he lives at Brighton. I met him at Assuan when I went on board to see if they had a book on board I wanted.

I don't think I have any more news for you at present. It has been very chilly at night since we came here and even in the day it has never been very hot. I hope by now you have received my latest batch of letters from Assuan. Yours received yesterday dated 13th–14th Jan. only speaks of receiving my 1st letter from Wadi Halfa on the way up. But I expect I shall hear from you on Friday or Saturday. I look forward to your letters very much although I don't say much about them in mine. The reason being as I have mentioned before, that you naturally prefer to have my news and not comments on yours. I was glad to know that Violet enjoyed getting my letter. We had a man and his wife named Alexander to lunch yesterday. I don't know who they are but they came out in one of those new steamers and she has lost her trunks and all her dresses and they <u>say</u> they never put them ashore. I dare say you saw there was a strike of stokers who got at the champagne and all got drunk and one stole some clothes out of a passenger's cabin. The waiters too being hotel waiters were all sea sick! So there was no one to wait.

Much love to you darling and the chicks. Also to No. 10 remember me to the Hamptons and "absent friends".

Your loving husband
Ferdy
A.F.R. Platt

SS *Serapis* Luxor
Friday Jan. 24th 1908

My dearest,

First of all many thanks for your letter and the weekly *Times*, and all your news. I was very glad Violet and Boy both went to the Wilmers' and enjoyed themselves so much.

And now about Erny's letter which I enclose. I am dreadfully grieved to think he should have had all this trouble. It is indeed unfortunate that he has not been able to get out to India as he hoped. After reading his letter you will not feel surprised when I ask you to send him a cheque at once. I have written by this mail saying that you will send him one for seventy pounds but I should like to send him one for a hundred if you think we can do so, as things seem to be very serious for him just now. I am afraid Minnie must have felt very sad at the time of her confinement and ever since then events must have added to her anxiety. With her bringing up I should imagine that she is not the best manager of domestic affairs. I don't know what will happen if he is ordered to S. Africa or Gibraltar. It is very sad. I hope when I get home on the 15th that I shall find a letter from him or that he has written to you to say how things are going on.[1]

I have very little news. I went over to Medinet Habu with the Duke and the others and took them to Carter's house after they had seen the tomb of Nefert-Ari and the Duke bought two of his best sketches, a head of Seti I at Abydos and Queen Nefert-Ari from her tomb. I only wish I could have them. He has promised to send me a little sketch later on. I have been to Karnak twice and I think I told you that I climbed to the top of the

---

1   The anxiety in Erny's household was probably caused by the lack of opportunities for a young infantry officer, quite recently married with two small children, to gain promotion in peacetime and thereby a reasonable income. Minnie's "bringing up" was as the daughter of Randolph Innes-Hopkins, a wealthy Yorkshire industrialist with numerous servants, and she did later receive a reasonable inheritance. Her sadness may also have resulted from her father's death and her own family's adversities. Later Erny did achieve command of his regiment in India, where he and Minnie spent most of the years of the First World War—separated however from their sons, who remained with foster parents in England.

mountain at the back of Deir el Bahri (about 1,000 feet high), before I had lunch with Carter. Otherwise I have no news. I am absolutely yearning to get out of this boat. I sympathize with my brother medical man in Macbeth and can say with him,

> Were I from Dunsinane away and clear
> Profit again would hardly draw me here.[1]

Sir C.H., who only cares for "huntin'" and cards, told me he was never so bored in his life. He must be! You can't imagine what a deadly dull time we have on board. However I will describe my experiences when I can use my tongue and not my pen.

With regard to your mother's wish to have a piece of native jewelry there does not seem to be any native jewelry as far as I can see. Most things seem to be made abroad, and the little shops are full of Birmingham rubbish, Italian jewelry such as that I bought for you at the Italian Exhibition at Earls Court. I have bought some things however and although it is the work of the needle I hope she won't feel very disappointed. This country is the most disappointing place to buy things in.

Much love to you darling and the children and No. 10.

Ever your affectionate husband
A.F.R. Platt
(Ferdy)

We leave here for Cairo tomorrow and instead of leaving them here I shall probably leave them at Cairo or possibly but <u>not</u> probably at Assyut. I enclose a cheque from the Duchess for £110. Will you pay it in for me and then draw cheque for Erny?

---

1   Lines from Shakespeare's *Macbeth*, Act V Scene 3.

SS *Serapis* near Balyāna
Monday Jan. 27th 1908 11.30 AM

My dearest,

We left Luxor at 7.45 am yesterday (Sunday). It was very cold with a strong west or S.W. wind blowing and we sat down to lunch with overcoats and caps. It was so cold and rough that we tied up at a place called Deshna at 2 o'clock and stayed there till 7.45 this morning. The sky was covered with clouds and after lunch while Sir C. and I were out for a walk it rained a little. Great clouds of dust were blowing all day. In the evening I went for another brisk walk with Lord G. and came home feeling quite warm. I wore my blue suit all day and at night I put on warmer under clothing; after dinner it became colder and colder and although I had a coat on and rug over my feet I thought bed would be the best place so I went! 2 blankets a rug and dressing gown. This morning at 7.20 my thermometer was only 45°F! So I put on my thick brown suit and my thick striped waist coat. Dining room was only 47°F when I had my breakfast. I had a smart tramp after breakfast up and down the deck feeling frisky in the cold air. I did so yesterday too.

About an hour ago we had some excitement as we ran on a sand bank and had to be pulled off by hauling on the anchor which was taken out in the boat and dropped overboard. As there is less cloud today it is getting warmer and the wind is at present not quite so strong as yesterday although the river is covered with waves. This wind began to get up in the early morning yesterday and woke me up by blowing the canvas about which is put up all round the boat. It sounded like hundreds of umbrellas being opened and shut quickly. This cold weather reminds me of home and I am quite glad, in a way, to be so reminded. If it continues till I leave Egypt I shall not find much difference when I get on board the *Mongolia*. I am going all the way down to Cairo on board and stay here until I go on Monday the 3rd just a week today. I expect we shall get to Cairo about the 30th. I shall only get two more letters from you before I leave. But I shall post this and two more I hope. I shall also post at Marseilles and Gibraltar if possible. The Duchess told me that the *Mongolia* is a fine boat. Much bigger and better than the one we came out in. This morning we passed <u>under</u> the railway bridge at Nagh Hamadi as the Nile is much lower of course than when we went up. So we did not have to wait till it was opened. The day before we left Luxor (Sat. 25th I posted a letter to you enclosing Erny's and a cheque from the Duchess) I met Whymper in the morning, who asked me to go his Dahabeyah and he gave me one of his sketches, because I helped him to tell his boy in Arabic to take a message over to the other side. The boat really belongs to another friend of his named Nicol, who speaks Arabic well but Whymper can't.

In the afternoon to my surprise Sir C. asked me to go over to the other side to the Valley of the Tombs of the Kings and see some puppies belonging to Ayrton. When we had rowed over he thought he would like to climb over the short path by Deir El Bahri instead of round the long road by donkey so we rode to the foot of the cliff and he started off at earnest pace up the steep stony path, which surprised me because for nearly three months he has hardly taken any exercise at all except to potter about the bazaars and "front" at Assuan and Luxor. Whereas I had been taking exercise on every possible occasion. I must explain to you that not only is the path very steep and rough but the sun was very hot and shining straight on our backs; it was less than an hour after lunch and he had been smoking. He has put on a lot [of] flesh and is a red-faced, thick-necked man. I found it very hard work and wondered how long I should be able to keep up the pace. However he soon stopped and said he felt sick so I made him lie down for a bit. After that I went in front and he walked [at] my pace! When we got to the bottom of the valley on the other side he asked Ayrton to send for the donkeys to come round and so ride all the way back. I was quite ready to walk back to them after tea the way we came so you see I am pretty fit.

The children would have been pleased to see the puppies playing about with the mother. They were born up there in that wild desolate valley. There were three of them and Sir C. took one. A man carried it down to the boat and it is now on board in its basket and in an empty champagne box. It is fed on bread and milk. I spent most of yesterday in reading through every letter I have received from you dearest, since I came to Egypt! I see in one you asked me whether Violet should eat honey. I should not let her have much especially if she has sugar in other things. Yes I did know that Lund's patient was dead. I think Lewis said so. Your father wanted to know if we chose our own drinks; we do. I generally have claret or hock but sometimes I have champagne because I am liable to get sour claret if it is opened for me today and I get it two days after!

You will guess now that the reason Erny and Minnie did not write to you this month was because of all this worry. You mentioned in one of your letters that they had a nurse girl as well as the old one and that you thought they might have managed with one. What they ought to do is to get rid of the old one and get a good young nurse who will take both. As I said in my last I don't think Minnie is a good house manager and I don't think you do either. I am sorry I can't possibly hear from you or them until I get home unless I get a letter at Marseilles. I can't imagine how they will manage.

We have just (1.50 pm) arrived at Balyana and are going in to lunch.

6.10 pm – Just returned from a (second) visit to Abydos. We only went to the temple of Seti I but it is always worth seeing. We all went except Sir C. The Duchess and Lady G. drove. It is an 8-mile donkey ride but it was not so cold and there was no dust worth mentioning as the road runs through cultivated ground all the way. Coming home my donkey stumbled and fell and my donkey boy tried to save me but fell on the top of me: result – bruised ribs! The donkey stumbled again several times but didn't fall. However about a mile from the river I got off and walked the rest of the way. The donkeys get something the matter with their legs which I was told is peculiar to Egypt and has something to do with their feeding (or want of it?) and when they get the disease they are liable to go down.

It is much warmer this evening and the wind has dropped. Temp in my cabin 58°F. I wonder what Cooke-Hurle's wife died of and what has been the matter with McClellan Blair. I am so glad the chicks have had such a good time this Xmas. Give them both lots of kisses and love. I shall be so glad to see you all again. I am going to get this posted here in case of accidents.

Much love darling from your affectionate husband
Ferdy
A.F.R. Platt

Violet
xxxxxxxxx
xxxxxxxxx

Rowly
xxxxxxxxxxx
xxxxxxxxxxx

Sat. Feb. 1 1908

My dearest,

This is probably the last letter I shall write to you from Egypt – unless
there is something important to add.

Yesterday 31st Jan. we could not start till 9.45 owing to a thick mist.
Then sometime after we did get off we had to tie up at the bank for an hour
as the chain of the condensor pump broke. The Duke, Sir C. and I went
on shore and had coffee in the house of the local Omdeh or governor. He
is a rich man, owns some 500 acres, which means £20 or £30 an acre! Last
night we tied up at the bank a few miles below Rigga or Rikka. There was
a fine sunset which formed a grand background for the great Pyramid of
Medum which rose from the plain in mysterious solitude. We were quite
near the railway and although we couldn't see it, the sound of the trains
reminded me of the suburbs of London.

This morning there was another thick mist which delayed us until after
10 o'clock. The dining room was only 45°F at 8.30. We expect to get to
Cairo about 2 or 3 o'clock just too late to go to the Museum. I shall have
to go to Cooks, though, to get my ticket and money in exchange for Cook's
draught. I had a draught from them at Assuan in exchange for one of the
Duchess's cheques. This delay in getting to Cairo is disappointing as I did
hope to see something of the Museum. I shall only have tomorrow Sunday.
On Monday I leave Cairo by the 11 am train for Port Said. Mon. Feb. 3
for P&O *Mongolia*

Cairo at last!

We arrived here about 3 o'clock this afternoon and Sir C. and I walked
across the Kasr El Nil Bridge[1] into Cairo to Cooks office where I changed
my draught and bought my ticket (cost of which the Duchesses added
to her cheque) we then went to Shepheard's Hotel where I had tea and
after buying a few things we walked back to the boat. I have to post this

---

1   The bridge connecting the island of Gezira with Tahrir Square in downtown Cairo.

by 9 or 10 tomorrow morning to catch the Brindisi mail so I am writing in my cabin (having just finished dinner). I am going off to the Museum tomorrow morning about 9 o'clock. We arrived so late this afternoon that it was not worth while going to the Museum as it closes at 4.30. You can imagine how disappointed I am at not being able to spend more time there.

Every one is glad the trip is over. . . . Sir C. wishes he could come back by my boat. Lord G. said if he had known what it was going to be he would not have brought his boat etc., etc.! Cairo looks very different now to what it did when we arrived there at the end of October. There were very few people about then. It is now the height of the season and the place is crammed. Before we went into Cairo this afternoon the dragoman went off to Cooks to get our letters and we met him driving back so we stopped him and got our letters. I read yours in the street as I walked along! It is the last I shall get in Egypt! Thank you dearest for it and also for the one I had at Assyut also the weekly *Times* today. Tell Violet I was very pleased with her postcard and the bow wows. The puppy Sir C. brought from the Valley of the Tombs of the Kings at Thebes is doing well. He tries to bark now! Violet's idea of Thomas Cook and Son being the postman is a good one because that is just what they are! Funny to read about your fogs after writing about ours here!

Please thank your father for his advice about the way to get home from the docks. They tell me at Cook's that it depends upon the time the steamer arrives whether the train goes to Liverpool Street or Fenchurch St. As soon as I arrive I will send you a wire from the docks. I shall be very very glad to get home again and to see you and the children.

8am
I have to see his Grace this morning which means more delay and less time to spend in the Museum. No more now. Much love to you all kiss the children for me. Only 16 days now before I am home. Shall be glad to get there.

Your loving husband
A.F.R. Platt

Fri. Feb. 7 1908 – SS *Mongolia*

My dearest,

I am beginning this today as I am not quite certain what time we reach
Marseilles tomorrow. I have very little news for you dear as life on board
ship is not prolific of incidents and in addition I spent most of Tuesday and
Wednesday in bed owing to the weather dealing roughly with my Little
Mary!

My cabin is rather far forward. I selected it to get away from the noise
of the crew but I get the full height of the pitching. Yesterday the sea went
down and I went up! The stewards look after you very well when you are
sick and you can have any sort of food you fancy. But the tea and coffee
and milk are bad here as they were in Egypt. I am looking forward to a
nice cup of Cardena and some really good milk when I get home. We went
through the Straits of Messina yesterday by daylight. I was struck by the
wild rugged scenery on both the Italian and Sicilian side. The mountains
seem very high and broken up. I believe I saw Etna but am not sure. Soon
after passing the Straits the sunset but I was able to see the smoke coming
out of the top of Stromboli.[1] We passed it closely later on but it was then
too dark to see anything. There are not many people on board and there
will be an exodus at Marseilles tomorrow. I have not come across anyone I
care for my much, except a colonel whose name I don't know.

I am enjoying the sea air and hope to turn up looking well which I
certainly should not do after a night journey from Marseilles to Paris. I
hope you are all well. You can't imagine how I am longing to see you all. I
feel almost tempted to get off at Marseilles in spite of what I have written
above. Much love to you all. Big kisses to Violet and Boy.

Your loving and impatient husband
Ferdy

1　One of the Aeolian Islands off the north coast of Sicily, and an active volcano.

Sat. Feb. 8 1908 – SS *Mongolia*, Marseilles

A great many passengers have left the ship today and it certainly does seem silly to think that they will be in London tomorrow and I shall be another week on the way. However, I shall miss that ghastly railway travelling at night in a horrible stuffy Wagon Lit.

I met a man who has just left the ship. He is on leave from China and is in the Consular Service at Shanghai. He was in the Siege of the Legation at Peking[1] and knows Mrs. Lemon. Lemon has had a row with his superior and has either been kicked out or resigned. But this man says it is always easy to get a job in China so I hope for her sake that he has by this time. We have a varied assortment of people on board. Man and wife I went out with are quite young and come from Edinburgh. They came from Cairo by same train that I did. They did not care for Egypt but as they merely staid in Cairo they did not see much. There is a big colonial bishop with a big voice, big daughter and wife. It was very cold this morning until the sun was high. I am writing this in what is called the music room with an oval hole in the floor looking down into the dining room and a barrel roof with glass in big squares, the frame work of which is gilded. The panels of the room are oak with soft green curtains, tablecloths and upholstery. At each end of barrel is a picture in fresco – railways round oval opening in floor and six thin columns which support roof. There is a big smoking room.

Well darling this day week will see me home and very glad I shall be. I was vexed I could not get anything in Cairo on Sunday all the shops were shut. I have nothing for boy, and did not see anything in Marseilles today either.

I hope I shall manage something at Gib. Much love Darling to you and the children.

Ever your loving husband
Ferdy

---

1   The Siege of the International Legations took place in Peking (Beijing) in the summer of 1900 during the Boxer Rebellion. Some 900 military and civilian personnel from Europe, Japan, and the USA, together with about 2,800 Chinese Christians, took refuge in the Legation Quarter of Peking, where they survived a 55-day siege by a Chinese government force and its allies. The siege was lifted by the arrival of an international military force which defeated the Chinese army and occupied the city.

4

The World beyond 1908

The Future Lives of the Passengers

The last days of the duke

Ferdy had been appointed specifically to attend to the duke's health for the duration of his journey on the Nile. On Monday, February 3, 1908, therefore, having completed the assignment and anxious to return to the home comforts of London, he took leave of his employers and departed Cairo.

The duke's party was to prolong its stay in Egypt, however. The only clue as to why this was is provided for by a series of letters, in the Devonshire Archives at Chatsworth,[1] written from the Grand Hotel Helouan between February 20 and 26 by Eddy Stanley, the duchess's son-in-law, who was married to Alice, Louisa Gosford's sister. It would appear that while in Cairo the duke's health had worsened dramatically, and that Lord Stanley, later to be the politician the Earl of Derby, had arrived from England to provide additional familial support.

Stanley wrote a series of long letters home to Alice, protesting how valuable his presence was—possibly to offset his occasional enjoyment of the Cairo attractions of golf and racing. His descriptions of the state of the duke and his party, three weeks after Ferdy's departure, suggest what a forlorn and fractious group they had become, as the duke's health fluctuated daily. He wrote in his first letter, referring to the duke as the more familiar "Lord Hartington":

Lord Stanley (17th Earl of Derby)

Lord Stanley, portrait by William Orpen

Lord Stanley (1865–1948), English soldier and statesman, grandson of the 14th Earl of Derby who served three times as prime minister of the United Kingdom. Stanley had already established himself in public life by 1908, having served for ten years as a professional soldier with the Grenadier Guards and subsequently as private secretary to Field Marshal Lord Roberts in the Second Boer War. Stanley succeeded to the earldom of Derby, subsequently serving twice as secretary of state for war, and then as ambassador to France. Outside politics, he was best known in racing circles, and was one of the most prominent owner–breeders of the first half of the twentieth century. He had twenty classic winners, including three Epsom Derbys (a race named after his forebear, the 12th Earl of Derby), all no doubt made possible by an annual rental income from the ancestral estates equivalent today to seven million pounds a year.

Much as I hated coming I am pleased that I did – as I think it really was appreciated not only by Louise but by Lord Hartington. Her Grace was pleased – but less pleased than when a telegram was given her this morning to say that Cassel was coming at 4 o'clock this afternoon to see her! Gosford and Theo met me in Cairo and I got from them an idea of how things were – but it was not till I got here that I really appreciated all that they had gone through. I should think that the Nile trip had been a perfect hell on earth. Louise looking ten years older.

Until one has seen the doctor one does not realise how bad Lord H has been and to my mind still is. On Saturday morning the doctor told me that he didn't think he could live but he suddenly made a marvellous rally – but even now he is getting three times a day the very strongest dose of strychnine that a doctor is allowed to give and therefore his strength is really ficticious and it remains to be seen what the effect of leaving off the dose will be.

Following the passing of another attack:

> I had a long talk with him this morning about every sort of thing – in
> the middle he suddenly said "How does the doctor think he is going to
> tell me how shall I die?"
>
> Later on he talked for a long time about politics etc. and this even-
> ing played two rubbers of bridge & is quite another man. But my dear,
> what they have been through during these last five months – it must
> have been hell. There is only one description possible of their Graces
> – it is a d——d cantankerous old couple.

Stanley notes wryly that the social proclivities of the Double Duchess
remain undiminished:

> Her Grace is very cheery though. She has been into Cairo to have
> luncheon with Cassel – don't tell Charlie [her son Lord Charles Mon-
> tagu] all this – only tell him that he may have to come out here if by any
> chance they are not able to leave for home on the 12th, but I am not
> afraid now that they will not be able to do so.
>
> Tonight Sir William dined here. He certainly is the most delightful of
> men. Louise was a little foolish about him at dinner – he sat between
> her and her Grace & she entirely monopolized him talking Egyptology
> – which she knows her Grace hates. It very evidently made her Grace
> cross!

Stanley berates the duchess for:

> her longing for home – or rather society – which is quite extraordinary.
> It is absolute madness coming north so soon and Lord H didn't want
> to come – but she absolutely insisted and wouldn't stop a minute any-
> where. What the Gosfords have been through passes belief.
>
> [. . .]
>
> Mind you impress upon Charlie that at Cannes Lord H must lead an
> absolutely invalid life. There will be no question of driving out although
> a little bridge before dinner – but he must not be in a room with anybody
> sickening.

The duke's state of health changes by the day, but writes Stanley:

> I am not staying on his account but for the others. You have <u>no</u> idea of the state they are all in – Lord Hartington is one of the most damnably cantankerous old men I have ever met. His ingratitude is extraordinary and only equaled by his grumbling. He is beastly to her Grace – she in turn vents it on the rest. Gosford is never spoken to at all, even if he asks either of them a question, there is no answer. Louise's nerves are quite gone . . . even Theo is all on wires.

Finally Stanley marvels at the duke's constitution, before saying that he could not "see the <u>slightest</u> reason why he should not sail on the 11th – a nurse goes with him." He then ends this final letter to Alice, as he invariably did, with "Best love old girl to you, Victoria & my dog."

The death and funeral of the duke

The end for the duke was to come not in Egypt, but very shortly thereafter. He made his journey with the duchess to France but did not get further than Cannes and the Metropole Hotel, which had been a favorite of his over the years. He died there on March 24, 1908. As he lay unconscious he was heard to mutter, as though playing at cards, "Well, the game is over, and I am not sorry."[2]

The duke's coffin was then carried from the Riviera to Derbyshire, and after lying for a day and a night "covered in the national flag, and visited by all the retainers of the estates, was buried on the 28th March on the rising ground in the beautiful churchyard of Edensor, within the Park of Chatsworth." The duchess had suffered a bad fall on returning home but insisted on being present at the funeral, wheeled in a Bath chair up the incline and then standing at the graveside supported on one side by the new duke and the other by her son "Charlie" Montagu and Eddy Stanley. Among the wreaths in her view was one from the queen bearing the inscription "In remembrance of our dear Duke of Devonshire, in deepest sorrow and regret, from Alexandra."

The duchess received many messages of condolence. While she was still in Cannes, telegrams arrived in care of the Metropole Hotel from around the world—among them, from Edward R. and Alexandra (King Edward VII and Queen Alexandra) in Biarritz, Alfonso (King Alfonso XIII of Spain) from the Palacio in Madrid, Leopold (King Leopold II) of the Belgians in Bruxelles,

Arthur Balfour[3] in London, Consuelo Marlborough in New York, Nellie Melba in Napoli, and Alice Keppel (one of King Edward VII's mistresses) also in Biarritz (no doubt because the king was there).

Among the many letters the duchess received at Chatsworth, and which remain there in the family archives, is one from the king, but there were also three from correspondents who had seen the duke on his last voyage on the Nile: one from Winston Churchill, one from "Topps" care of London's Marlborough Club, and the third touchingly from the dragoman of the *Serapis*, Selim Gaziri, written on April 1, 1908, from the Mena House Hotel, Pyramids, Cairo, and addressed to "Her Grace the Most Venerable Duchess of Devonshire."

On the afternoon of the day when news had come of the duke's death, the two Houses of Parliament had been sitting, and in both Houses there had been orations in his honor and remembrance—recalling a character far removed from that of Eddy Stanley's "cantankerous old man." Reported in the House of Lords, among many others, Lord Roseberry[4] said:

It is not for me tonight to speak of him as a friend. He was the friend of many here. No more loyal friend, no more honest, no more unselfish and devoted friend could any man have . . . He was the best and most generous of landlords; he was a high-minded, enthusiastic sportsman; he was a devoted husband; he was kind to all with whom business or society brought him into contact; and he was the most generous of hosts. But there have been many in his high position who have been all these things, and many who have shared with him the title in which I think he would have taken the most pride – that of being an English gentleman. More than that he was one of the great reserve forces of this country.

In the Commons, Mr. Asquith[5] is reported in Hansard as saying:

In the Duke of Devonshire we have lost almost the last survivor of our heroic age . . . There has been no more splendid example in our time of service which can be rendered to the State by simplicity of nature, sincerity of conviction, directness of purpose, intuitive insight into practical conditions, quiet and inflexible courage and above all, I would say, tranquil indifference to praise and blame, and by absolute disinterestedness.

Ferdy may have seen evidence of these characteristics in the tired old man he nurtured through his last journey on the Nile. In his letters there appear glimpses, on both sides, of the very restrained affection permitted by propriety.

Members of the duke's party in later life

The duchess herself lived on until 1911, increasingly frail but with the devoted support of her son Lord Charles Montagu. Although she traveled abroad frequently, she suffered a seizure as a result of the heat nearer home, at Sandown Races on July 14. She died the following day, a year after King Edward VII, with whom she and the duke had shared such a colorful life.

The Gosford family did not appear to prosper in the years that followed. The earl had been a member of the inner circle of the Prince of Wales and Lord of the Bedchamber when the prince ascended the throne as King George V. The need to finance the lavish lifestyle of a member of the king's inner circle caused the earl to plunder the family finances, and a racing debt led to the sale of the contents of the library at Gosford Castle, County Armagh, built up by the efforts of his ancestors—and now largely, as these things go, in the ownership of the Pierpont Morgan Library in New York. The remaining contents of the house were sold in 1921 and the earl died the following year.

Perhaps unpredictably, as far as Ferdy was concerned, the future star of the party was to be Lady Theodosia. She did not of course fulfil her engagement to the Hon. Thomas Agar-Robartes, but instead in August 1912 married the Hon. Alexander George Montagu Cadogan, youngest son of the Fifth Earl Cadogan.

Alexander Cadogan was to become one of the most important diplomats and civil servants of his time. As permanent under-secretary for foreign affairs from 1939 to 1946, he was one of the central figures of British policy before and during the Second World War. He was highly regarded by Churchill, who said that "His Majesty's Government could have no abler representative than Sir Alexander Cadogan,"[6] and who in the 1950s appointed him chairman of the BBC.

Lady Theo would have therefore spent much time with Winston Churchill, whom she first encountered on the Nile with her grandmother, the great society hostess. According to the *Oxford Dictionary of National Biography*, "Theo Cadogan was a lady of highly individual character, who exercised great influence in family matters without intrusion into official business, and the marriage was extremely happy." When Sir Alexander was the United Kingdom's first permanent representative to the United Nations, he and Theo cultivated a large and varied number of friends by entertaining at their Long Island home, Hillandale. Her grandmother would doubtless have been proud. Outliving Alexander by ten years, and survived by her four children, Theo Cadogan died in 1977.

Sir Charles Cradock-Hartopp's letter of condolence to the duchess strikes a rather awkward note. He had evidently been at his friend's burial, for he writes "I know myself I was deeply affected at Chatsworth and I was so sorry for you," and goes on to say that he had made three attempts at writing to her. It would seem unlikely that he would continue to be a visitor to Chatsworth after the duke's death. He is recorded as being a justice of the peace for Warwickshire, but there is no other evidence of significant public duty. He never remarried and died childless in 1929. The baronetcy, after passing through various cousins, is now extinct.

Ferdy's latter years

After the excitement of the Nile trip, Ferdy appears to have lived a largely uneventful life, at least as far as the outside world was concerned. He was too old for the Great War, the cataclysmic event which would change forever the Edwardian era of imperial security, privilege, and deference to which his letters were witness. Not long after the troubled peace that followed, he and May escaped from the smog and urban clang of London's Maida Vale to the tranquility of the village of Underriver near Sevenoaks in Kent.

Ferdy's inner world, always centered on his love of Egyptology, appears to have been as tranquil as the countryside around him. He is known by his family to have translated the Book of Genesis into Egyptian hieroglyphics—almost certainly the only person to have done so! He was also a sensitive watercolorist of landscapes and intimate domestic still lifes. He died quietly in 1946.

There had however been one family tragedy late in his life that may have turned him further inward. After Eton and the Royal Agricultural College, his son Rowley had emigrated to the colony of Kenya in East Africa, where he had bought a highland farm close to Subukia. Ferdy must have visited him there, because there is a watercolor of the view from his farm, through the eucalyptus trees to the Rift Valley below. Rowley had married inappropriately at a difficult time in the colony's social history, and he died unhappily by his own hand in 1942.

After London University, Violet, the childhood recipient of Ferdy's box, spent some years in Kenya herself, and the only evidence of romance in her life, with a Czech settler, came from that time. She also encountered in Kenya the movement of the moment, which was to dominate her life: Moral Re-Armament (or MRA).[7] When not looking after her widowed mother she was to work with much dedication for Frank Buchman, its American founder, and was a frequent visitor to its center at Caux, in Switzerland.

Violet died in 1992, passing her father's Egyptian letters, and the precious box he had created for her, to succeeding generations.

The Future of Egypt and
Its Archaeologists

Egypt in transition

Ferdy's letters from Egypt, written in the winter of 1907–1908, chronicle a country in transition. Life along the banks of the Nile, little changed since the days of the pharaohs, was undergoing rapid change in the face of modern technology and the economic development unleashed by the British colonial authorities. Some visitors, like the Oxford professor Archibald Sayce, who had wintered in Egypt for many years, were dismayed at the changes as they felt a timeless world slipping away. Others, with their eyes fixed firmly on the future, were optimistic about the improvements that modernization would bring to Egypt and its inhabitants. While Lady Theo indulged in the newfangled hobby of photography, Ferdy recorded his observations in words, his letters providing a fascinating firsthand account of the projects and people who would shape Egypt and change its way of life forever.

There were still timeless vistas to enjoy, and Ferdy described these with great sensitivity:

"The bright sun, blue sky, the limestone cliffs, the *shadufs*, the women filling and carrying their water jars on their heads, the various birds. . . .

131

Then there are the sunsets and brilliant stars. Last night a magnificent meteor fell in front of us and seemed to explode into pieces, its reflexion in the water was pretty."

But the modern world was intruding fast. At Esna, the party disembarked to inspect the barrage being built across the Nile to regulate the river's flow and increase the area of cultivable land. The scale of the project was immense, employing up to twelve thousand men. The contract was held by the Scottish engineering firm of John Aird, and the European supervisors drove their Egyptian workers hard—finishing the job a year early would suit "not only J. Aird & Co but also the Government because whenever this is done they get the value of a whole extra year's crop." While the government inspector had "a nice house, very high rooms and cool," the long-suffering workers could look forward to a sports match at Christmas in which they could win "a few piastres in an obstacle race or for climbing a greasy pole."

More irrigation works were taking place further south, at Kom Ombo, largely to benefit the British industrialist Sir Ernest Cassel, who had purchased vast tracts of land to grow cotton. The project was overseen by the government engineer Sir William Willcocks, who had something of a checkered career and ended his days, ruined and disgraced, after falling out with his fellow experts on the most appropriate design for the Aswan Dam. From Ferdy's letter, we learn that Willcocks had been no stranger to hardship, having suffered blood poisoning in Uganda leading to facial paralysis. The British Empire seemed to produce such men, determined, self-assured, and indefatigable in the face of adversity.

At Aswan, Ferdy found the town itself "much improved," with several new hotels (notably the Cataract) strung out along the newly constructed corniche, to cater for the increasing number of tourists. Tourism was also changing Egyptian culture, and Ferdy bemoaned the paucity of native crafts in the bazaars: "Most things seem to be made abroad and the little shops are full of Birmingham rubbish." Visitors to Egypt today might make the same observation, replacing "Birmingham" with "China."

By far the most radical transformation, on Aswan and the whole of the Nile Valley, was being wrought a few miles to the south of the city, at the foot of the First Nile Cataract. Here the Aswan Dam, finished as recently as 1902, was about to be raised in height, with far-reaching consequences. The beautiful temple of Philae was already submerged, "looking quite sad and out of place in all these horribly modern surroundings," while nearby burials had been "quite spoilt by the damp and infiltration of water." Ferdy was prescient when he wrote, "Every perishable thing in a tomb has been or eventually will be destroyed, if that tomb happens to be in a spot which is now below or near the present high water mark – Dam!" The irrigation works were also wreaking irreparable damage to the natural ecosystem—Ferdy recorded "dead or dying pelicans all the way up beyond the dam"—and to human lives, displacing countless people. He wrote, rather laconically, "In three years' time when the dam is completed the water will be 17 feet higher and then they will have to clear out."

Ferdy's letters are perhaps the last extended, firsthand account of the sights of Upper Egypt and Lower Nubia before they changed, or disappeared, forever.

Endings and beginnings

The changes that Ferdy observed during his visit of 1907–1908 gathered pace in the years that followed. The First World War, which in Europe ushered in the demise of the old aristocratic order, was in Egypt marked by the awakening of nationalist sentiment. This was both a reaction to British occupation (declared at the end of 1914) and to the burden shouldered by Egypt as part of the war effort—which included the conscription of over one-and-a-half million Egyptians, and the requisitioning of crops, livestock, and buildings to supply the British army. Shepheard's Hotel, for example, served as the army's headquarters in the Near East. In 1919, resentment came to a head, sparking a countrywide revolution against British rule. The colonial authorities found themselves powerless to restrain Egypt's longing for self-determination, and in 1922 acquiesced in the proclamation of Khedive Fuad as king of an independent Egypt.

However, certain matters were still reserved to the British government, acting through its high commissioner (from 1936, ambassador), Lord Cromer. They included defense, communications, and the protection of Britain's interests in Egypt and the Sudan, notably control of the Suez Canal. These reserve powers enabled Britain to continue to administer Egypt during the Second World War, when the country played a pivotal role in the Allied effort, and the reoccupation of Cairo by British soldiers, spies, and bureaucrats almost seemed to turn the clock back to Edwardian days.

But the flame of nationalism was not so easily dampened, and in 1952 the increasingly unpopular British-backed Egyptian monarchy was deposed.

In the unrest, British interests across Egypt were attacked, symbolized most powerfully by the burning down of Shepheard's Hotel, for so long the cultural epicenter of British influence. A few weeks later, King Farouk sailed into exile, and Colonel Nasser was to become Egypt's new leader—the first native Egyptian to rule over the Nile Valley since the days of the pharaohs. Within a few years, the remaining traces of British colonial authority were systematically dismantled. The site of the British army barracks in the center of Cairo was closed and redeveloped; the Suez Canal was nationalized; even the gardens of the British ambassador's residence were forfeit to make way for the construction of the corniche road. Egypt had thrown off the shackles of colonial rule and was forging its own destiny as an Arab nation.

Two construction projects epitomized this new era in Egypt's history. The first was the establishment, on the site of the former British army barracks, of the first international hotel in the Middle East, the Nile Hilton. Occupying a prominent position on Tahrir Square, next to the Egyptian Museum of antiquities, the "Hilton slab" proclaimed Egypt as a forward-looking nation, eager to embrace modernity and to be part of an international order that looked beyond the old European powers. The Nile Hilton was opened in 1958 by President Nasser, its "pharaonic chic" aesthetic celebrating Egypt's historic greatness in a modern idiom, and setting the seal on a new center for Cairo. It rapidly became the hotel of choice for Western tourists and archaeologists alike, replacing Shepheard's as the lively hub of gossip in Egypt's capital.

The second development, taking place at about the same time, was the construction of the High Dam at Aswan, supplanting the old stone British barrage with a modernist concrete edifice funded by the Soviet Union. Begun in 1960 and opened in July 1970, the dam created Lake Nasser, flooding the settlements and archaeological sites of Nubia, and also prevented cruise ships from sailing upstream beyond Aswan. It thus marked the end of the classic Nile cruise from Cairo to Wadi Halfa. In place of well-heeled Edwardian trips "a thousand miles up the Nile," Egypt embraced a new era of mass-market tourism. Colonial watering holes gave way to glitzy international hotels, and polished wooden *dahabiya*s with shaded verandas were replaced by multidecker tourist cruisers with floor-to-ceiling picture windows.

Only in the twenty-first century did *dahabiya*s make a small-scale return to the Nile, prompted by a wider nostalgia for the glamour of the Gilded Age. Today, the clientele is altogether less aristocratic, the dress code less formal, and the manners less rigid; but, drifting with the current past timeless sandstone ruins, past farmers on donkeys, and egrets among the reeds, it is not difficult to be transported back a century ago, to an Edwardian sunset on the Nile.

Egyptologists and amateurs

As for the Egyptologists encountered by Ferdy during his 1907-to-1908 trip, theirs was a lasting legacy, for they helped to shape the future of the discipline for the rest of the twentieth century and beyond.

James Quibell, whom Ferdy met at Saqqara at the start of his voyage, went on to serve as director of the Egyptian Museum in Cairo from 1914 to 1923, and head of the Antiquities Service until his retirement in 1925. Arthur Weigall, who in 1907 had only recently replaced Howard Carter as chief inspector of antiquities for Upper Egypt, devoted himself as much to protection and conservation as to excavation, recognizing the threats posed to Egypt's ancient heritage by the country's accelerating modernization. The pressure took its toll, however, and Weigall suffered a breakdown. He left Egypt and spent the First World War in London as a set designer for the London stage, later becoming film critic for the *Daily Mail*. By a curious twist of fate, his journalistic career brought him back to Egypt to report on the opening of the tomb of Tutankhamun in 1922. The archaeological discovery of the century was a triumph, not for Weigall, but for the very man he had replaced, Howard Carter. Realizing that the world of archaeology now lay behind him, Weigall returned to the world of the theater as a writer of lyrics, and died in 1934.

Edward Ayrton's years at Thebes, working for Theodore Davis, were extraordinarily productive, culminating in the discovery of the royal tomb of Horemheb just a few months after Ferdy's visit. Ayrton went on to excavate at Abydos before accepting a position with the Archaeological Survey of Ceylon. It was a fateful decision. In May 1914, aged just 31, Ayrton drowned while on a shooting expedition in southern Ceylon. By contrast, Alan Gardiner went on to become one of the giants of twentieth-century Egyptology. In 1914, he was instrumental in establishing the *Journal of Egyptian Archaeology* as the principal academic periodical of British Egyptology, and his philological expertise made him the obvious choice to work on the inscriptions from the tomb of Tutankhamun. The publication, in 1923, of Gardiner's magisterial *Egyptian Grammar* remains a landmark in the study of the ancient Egyptian language. Equally influential was his 1961 book, *Egypt of the Pharaohs*, which remained the classic text on pharaonic history for the best part of half a century.

The memorial postcard issued for the funeral of the 8th Duke of Devonshire

George Andrew Reisner, whom Ferdy met at Aswan, ranks alongside Gardiner as a great figure in Egyptology, and the leading American Egyptologist of the twentieth century. His notable discoveries include the tomb of Queen Hetepheres and the magnificent statues of King Menkaura at Giza. At the time of Ferdy's visit, Reisner was director of the archaeological survey of Nubia for the Egyptian government. He subsequently explored the pyramids of Meroë and the temple at Napata, further south in Sudan, and can be credited with establishing the subdiscipline of Nubian archaeology. In 1910, Reisner was appointed curator of Egyptian collections at the Boston Museum of Fine Arts, remaining there until his death in 1942. He transformed the museum into one of the world's great repositories of Egyptian antiquities and a major international center of scholarship on pharaonic civilization.

Elliot Smith, while primarily an anatomist, played a prominent role in early twentieth-century discoveries, and was appointed adviser to the archaeological survey of Nubia. He was the first scientist to use x-rays to study Egyptian mummies nondestructively, and took a special interest in the human brain, becoming the leading specialist of his day. His theories on the evolution of the primate brain remain core to current scholarship. Shortly after Ferdy's visit,

Smith was appointed to the chair of anatomy at Manchester, subsequently transferring to the chair at University College London. In 1923, he was called upon to conduct the forensic examination of Tutankhamun's mummy. From 1924 to 1927 Smith served as president of the Anatomical Society of Great Britain and Ireland. It is tempting to think that his and Ferdy's paths may have crossed again, in London medical circles.

As for Howard Carter, his career in the years after 1908 has gone down in the annals of world archaeology. Irascible but brilliant, difficult but determined, he was the perfect choice to lead Lord Carnarvon's excavations in the Valley of the Kings, and was rewarded for years of seemingly fruitless work by the discovery of the intact tomb of Tutankhamun in November 1922. The discovery marked at once the culmination of Egyptology's golden age and its ending. It was immediately clear to Carter that the analysis of so vast and diverse a treasure could no longer be accomplished by a single scholar. Instead, a large team of experts, each with a different specialism, was required to do the find justice. The days of the archaeological polymath, together with those of the aristocratic patron, were over. From that moment on, the study of ancient Egypt would be more scientific, but also more remote. Egyptology in the second half of the twentieth century became as dry and dusty as the Valley of the Kings. The Egypt Exploration Society tolerated members of the general public as supporters, while excluding them from active involvement in the subject.

But, in the twenty-first century, as popular interest in ancient Egypt has undergone a renaissance, so has the participation of nonspecialists in the study and dissemination of pharaonic civilization. Popular Egyptological magazines hold their own alongside academic journals; regional societies fund excavations in the Nile Valley; enthusiastic amateurs once again have a voice and a contribution to make.

Ferdy Platt would be delighted.

Notes

1   All the letters quoted in this chapter are held at the Devonshire Archives at Chatsworth.
2   Vane, *Affair of State*, 247.
3   Arthur Balfour (1848–1930), English Conservative politician, and prime minister of the United Kingdom 1902–1905. He subsequently held many other important offices of state including foreign secretary (1916–19). In the latter capacity his name was given to the 'Balfour Declaration' which confirmed British support for the establishment in Palestine of a national home for the Jewish people.

4　Archibald Philip Primrose, 5th Earl of Roseberry (1847–1929), Scottish Liberal politician and prime minister of the United Kingdom 1894–95. He is thought to have preferred nonpolitical activities, and was an outstanding sportsman, as well as a writer and connoisseur. Winston Churchill, observing that Roseberry never adapted to democratic electoral politics, quipped, "He would not stoop; he did not conquer."

5　Herbert Henry Asquith (1852–1928), later ennobled as 1st Earl of Oxford and Asquith, English Liberal politician and prime minister of the United Kingdom 1908–16. He took the country into the First World War.

6　David Dilks, ed., *The Diaries of Alexander Cadogan* (New York: Putnam and Sons, 1972).

7　An international moral and spiritual movement launched in 1938 by Dr. Frank Buchman, as a successor to his Oxford Group, which achieved wide influence in the years of the Second World War and the ensuing peace.

Select bibliography

Bierbrier, M.L., ed. *Who Was Who in Egyptology*, 4th revised edition. London: The Egypt Exploration Society, 2012.

Dunn, W.E. Nickolls and George Vigers Worthington. *Luxor as a Health Resort*. London: H.K. Lewis, 1914.

Edwards, Amelia. *A Thousand Miles Up the Nile*. London: Century, 1982 (first published 1877).

Humphreys, Andrew. *Grand Hotels of Egypt in the Golden Age of Travel*. Cairo and New York: The American University in Cairo Press, 2011.

Humphreys, Andrew. *On the Nile in the Golden Age of Travel*. Cairo and New York: The American University in Cairo Press, 2015.

Manley, Deborah and Sahar Abdel-Hakim, eds. *Traveling Through Egypt from 450 BC to the Twentieth Century*. Cairo and New York: The American University in Cairo Press, 2004.

Reeves, Nicholas. *The Complete Tutankhamun*. London: Thames & Hudson, 1990.

Sayce, A.H. *Reminiscences*. London: Macmillan, 1923.

Thomas Cook & Son. *Programme of Cook's International Tickets to Egypt, Season 1887–88*. London: Thomas Cook & Son, 1887.

Vane, Henry. *Affair of State. A Biography of the 8th Duke and Duchess of Devonshire*. London: Peter Owen, 2004.

Wilkinson, Toby. *The Nile: Downriver Through Egypt's Past and Present*. London: Bloomsbury, 2014.

Willcocks, William. *Sixty Years in the East*. Edinburgh and London: William Blackwood and Sons, 1935.

Acknowledgments
and Illustration Credits

This book began to take shape in December 2012 when Toby Wilkinson, then Development Director of Clare College, Cambridge, led a group of the College's alumni on a voyage up the Nile in a *dahabiya*. During the trip, Ferdy's letters were read and the places he had visited were illuminated by Toby.

The authors wish to record their thanks to Medhat Saad, their authoritative and engaging tour guide, and their patient and attentive audience—Jonathan and Ann Goodridge, Claire Barnes, Laura Fan, Teresa Ma, Henry and Teresa Heuzenroeder, and Nigel and Judy Weiss.

I would particularly like to thank two former colleagues from Third Millennium: Neil Burkey, who provided support throughout the project, notably with picture research, and Matt Wilson, who designed the family trees and the map of the voyage. James Towe, the archivist and librarian, and Diane Naylor, the photo librarian for the Devonshire Collection at Chatsworth, were unfailingly helpful, as were the staff of the Churchill Archive at Churchill College, Cambridge. I would also like to thank my brother Nicholas Platt for his help, and finally my wife Amanda for participating in Ferdy's distant adventure for rather longer than she might have anticipated.

Julian Platt

Illustration credits

First plate section: The following are all copyright © by the Devonshire Collection, Chatsworth, and are reproduced by permission of the Chatsworth Settlement Trustees: the 8th Duke in Cannes; Hughes color portrait of the of the Duchess Louise; Chatsworth from the river with cattle in the foreground; shooting party with King Edward VII and the Duchess; 1897 costume ball (four pictures with the Duke and Duchess, Earl and Countess of Gosford); Sargent's portrait of the Acheson sisters; letter from Winston Churchill to the Duchess, August 1908; and the letter from the Duke to Alice Stanley, December 27, 1907. Winston Churchill's letter to the Dowager Duchess of Devonshire, August 18, 1908, has been reproduced with permission of Curtis Brown, London, © The Estate of Winston S. Churchill. The 'African Tour' photograph from the Churchill family album and the photograph taken by Churchill of the Duchess and party are reproduced with permission from Curtis Brown, London, on behalf of the Broadwater Collection. The photograph of Lady Theodosia with her husband Sir Alexander Cadogan is reproduced with the permission of Mr. and Mrs. David Coke.

Second plate section: All the images in this section are the copyright of Julian Platt and the Platt family with the exception of: Howard Carter's watercolor *Under the Protection of the Gods* © Bonhams 2001 2007; photograph of the SS *Serapis* on the Nile with two European passengers, reproduced with the permission of TopFoto; full length photograph of the SS *Serapis*, reproduced with permission of the Thomas Cook Archives.

Integrated images: Courtesy of the Rare Books and Special Collections Library, The American University in Cairo: pp 1, 13, 31, 121; © The National Portrait Gallery, London: pp. 22, 57, 69, 106; David Lyons / Alamy Stock Photo: p. 49; © 2007 Tufts University: p. 68; Fremantle /Alamy Stock Photo: p. 81; R. Neil Hewison: p. 101; Getty/Hulton Archive: p.108; Art Collection 2 / Alamy Stock Photo: p. 124; from the Devonshire Collection and reproduced with permission of the Chatsworth Settlement Trustees: p. 136.

Index